THE NEW CREATURES *and* MERE MEN

Kingsley Lawend

Copyright © 2024 Kingsley Lawend

All rights reserved. No part of this book may be reproduced, stored, or transmitted by any means—whether auditory, graphic, mechanical, or electronic—without written permission of both publisher and author, except in the case of brief excerpts used in critical articles and reviews. Unauthorized reproduction of any part of this work is illegal and is punishable by law.

Contents

Introduction 5
Chapter 1: The Creator of All Things 7
Chapter 2: Dominion 26
Chapter 3: Seeds 51
Chapter 4: The new 'gods" on earth 60
Chapter 5: Biblical Truths About The New
           Creatures 100
Prayer of Salvation 135

Introduction

Have you ever stopped to think about the remarkable transformation that takes place when you embrace life in Christ? In 2 Corinthians 5:17, the Bible reveals a truth that often goes unnoticed: when you come to Christ, you're not just changed; you're made entirely new. The old version of yourself is gone, making room for something extraordinary and divine—a life filled with remarkable potential, authority, and victory.

God's deepest desire is for all His children to live and relish the fullness of this life. In John 10:10 (AMPC), the Word of God reminds us that Jesus came to grant us this 'new' life and wants us to enjoy it as well.

This book has a specific purpose: to guide you in discovering and walking in the fullness of this beautiful life in Christ. We'll explore the differences between the natural man and the new man in Christ, the blessings that come from being born of divine origin, and the profound purpose behind your existence in Christ. The more you uncover, the more you'll be able to experience

INTRODUCTION

the reality of this life; for when you know it, you can see it, and when you see it, you can live it.

Welcome to 'New Creatures and Mere Men.' My prayer is that, through the inspiration of the Spirit of God, you'll not only grasp the depth of your purpose but also enjoy every moment of it.

Yours in Christ,
Kingsley Lawend

CHAPTER ONE

The Creator of All Things

God the Creator

God created all things by His will, design, and purpose. Some He created to only exist for a period of time, while others He created to exist eternally. Because He began the creation, no creation can give an account of the exact frame of eternity in which He began His creation. Often, people make reference to God as an eternal being. This is partially correct and also true. God is eternity; He dwells in eternity. He doesn't exist; He is existence. Therefore, He doesn't have life; He is life. If He had life, it would mean life was given to Him. But since He "is" the origin and source of all life, He is Life.

> *You are worthy, O Lord our God, to receive glory and honor and power. For you created all things, and they exist because you created what you pleased.* **Revelation 4:11 (NLT)**

He created what He pleased and how they pleased Him He created them. Since the emphasis of this book is on God's topmost of all creation, Man, we shall shed more light on who and what man is, who is he, why was he created, the old and the new man, and the responsibilities accorded to both the old and new man. Furthermore, we'll examine the reason God created man in His image and likeness and gave him authority over the works of His hands.

> *And he swore by Him who lives forever and ever, who created heaven and everything in it, the earth and everything in it, and the sea and everything in it; "There will be no more delay!"*
> **Revelation 10:6**

Before He created the heaven and everything in it, where was God, and how was He? From the Scriptures, we understand that God created Heaven, and all that is in it, first, before He created the earth, and everything that is in it. Now, it would be appropriate to conclude that there was nothing created before He created them, because He is before all things, whether in Heaven, on earth, or in the sea. Therefore, before He created all things, He was already God. The creation of all things didn't make Him God; He was already God before embarking on creation.

What is Man?

Only a few today would have adequate answers to this very significant question that has lingered for thousands of years. What man is, is clearly defined in Scriptures. In the Bible, the question, 'What is man?' is asked twice, first in Psalm 8 and repeated in the book of Hebrews, and then in Job 7. How do we define humanity, or what is a human being?

The best person to define a product would be the manufacturer, and besides, the manufacturer's definition of his product is more accurate than any other interpretation or definition. There are many worldly definitions of Man. Before we discover what the Bible's definition of man is, let's check out some worldly definitions of what man is.

Idealism

Idealism sees man as essentially a spiritual being, and his physical body is foreign to his essence. The body is nothing but a shell for the spirit or the intellect. Meaning:

- Man's body is neglected.
- Deeds done in the body do not pollute the essence of the person.
- Male/female identity is a biological mistake.

Materialism

Materialism concludes that man is composed of nothing more than material components. His intellectual, emotional, and spiritual aspects are seen as products of his material nature, operating under the rules of physics and biology. This perspective implies that:

- Man is not distinguished from other materials of creation. Consequently, man has no inherent dignity or worth, and it suggests that other animals or even plants have the same inherent worth as people.
- Man is not responsible for his behavior; instead, the environment is to be blamed for his unacceptable behavior.
- Man's identity is in no way related to God; therefore, man is, in some sense, ultimate.

All these definitions and descriptions of what man is do oppose the Christian view. From the Bible, we understand that Man is first spiritual and then material—together in perfect harmony. Furthermore, the Scriptures provide proper context of the Creator and creature relationship:

- Man is created and sustained by God who is the Creator of Man [Genesis 1:27, Acts 17:25, 28].
- Man is a person and is capable of making moral choices.
- Man is made in the image and likeness of his Creator, God [Genesis 1:27-28].

- Man's identity is due to the image of God he is created in.
- Man is God's representative [Genesis 9:6].
- Man resembles God [Genesis 1:26-31].
- Jesus Christ, God-Man, is the Perfect representative of what it means to be the image of God [2 Corinthians 4:3- 4, Colossians 1:15].

Thus, because of the fall of man, God's image in him is corrupted but not lost entirely [Psalm 58:3, Romans 5:12, Romans 8:7, 8, 1 Corinthians 2:14].

God Owns All

Behold all souls are Mine; the soul of the father as well as the soul of the son is Mine; the soul who sins shall die. **Ezekiel 18:20**

Because He created and formed all things, He owns them all. Therefore, all things must account to God, the Creator. He came up with all of the ideas, concepts, designs, purposes, and plans for creation. Despite many controversial arguments and scientific explanations of how all of these things came into being without a creator. It doesn't disapprove of the fact our Creator knows He created all things and that all things belong to Him.

The human race is the crowned Jewel of all His creation and everyone born into this world belongs to Him. Because He had a reason for creating everyone, no one human being came into planet Earth by accident or just coincidentally happened without His knowledge, purpose, and plan.

Since He created and owns all things, all things must gravitate and give their love and affection to Him. Unfortunately, this has not been the case, especially with His crowned jewel of creation—Man. Man has succeeded in deceiving himself into thinking that he created himself and that he has no one to be accountable to. The prophet Ezekiel reveals by the Spirit of God, God's conclusion on the matter, " All souls are Mine (God speaking), the soul of the father as well as the soul of the son is Mine, the soul that sins shall die. Meaning that all souls must account to Him alone, whether they agree, believe it or not.

> *But ask the animals, and they will teach you, or the birds in the sky, and they will tell you; or speak to the earth, and it will teach you, or let the fish in the sea inform you. Which of all these does not know that the hand of the Lord has done this? In His hand is the life of every creature and the breath of all mankind.* **Job 12:7-10 (NIV)**

According to the above Scripture, the animals, birds, and fishes know who created them, they all recognize His majestic power, and they know their place in creation. The argument that has lingered among the human race for thousands of years shouldn't be. Man couldn't have created himself; nothing would have been if man had such power to create himself, considering what man has done on the earth that was given to him to take care of, and how he has treated each other throughout his generations of existence. Thus, mankind should embrace the fact that God created them, in His image and likeness and this God is worthy of his life, service, and attention.

The Dust Man

From Genesis 1, we understand that man was made in the image and likeness of God. **Genesis 1:26-27**

In chapter 2, more details are revealed about the specifics of this creation. God created man out of matter or "the dust of the ground". So, man is a spirit entrapped in a dusty vessel called the body. His body is made from the most common material found in his environment, dust from the ground. Everything he wants, needs, and desires would have to come from the ground where his body was taken out from. Everything that has been invented, or will ever be invented, produced, or manufactured is in the earth, nothing comes from outside the earth. Even the Savior of mankind had to come from the earth. Because "dominion" was given to him, whatever he can think of in the earth realm will become so.

> *And the Lord God formed man out of the dust of the ground, and breathed into his nostrils the breath of life, and man became a living soul.*
> **Genesis 2:7**

The dustman was created as a living soul, his body gathered from the dirt of the earth was breathed into by God and He came alive. He was in a lifeless state until the breath of God entered his nostrils. It doesn't matter how dead or inactive a thing or situation is; when God breathes upon it, it comes alive. Imagine, everything man is came alive from just a breath from God. His body received blood, His brain and every other organ in his body began to function, and also his mind began to process thoughts. He was a dustman, anointed by the breath of God and nothing in the earth was left out under his dominion.

> *By the sweat of your brow, you will eat your bread, until you return to the ground—because out of it were you taken. For dust you are, and to dust you shall return.* **Genesis 3:19**

While judging Adam after he sinned, God reminded him where he was taken from, and reiterated that he would return to the same place as dust. Although he was taken from the dust, God's intention was not for him to go back into dust, but sin paved the way for the dustman to return to his environment.

> *All go to the same place; all come from dust; and to dust all return.* **Ecclesiastes 3:20 (NIV)**

Mere Men

Mere men are humans who are not functioning in the image and likeness of God, people who are not spiritually aligned with God by reason of the new birth. They are disconnected from the calling and purpose of God for their lives because they knowingly or ignorantly refuse to surrender themselves to their very source, God. Mere men are also those who have not come to the reality of who they are in God through Christ Jesus. Mere men can be poor, rich, wealthy, and influential in this world, but as long as they are not where they were created to be, they are common and mere mortals (dustmen).

Anyone without the Spirit of Christ in them is a mere man, a person who is ruled and controlled by their senses, and only relates to their senses, and cannot know the things of God, nor can they understand them. They are dead to God and cannot be in the kingdom of God until they repent and become born again, becoming new creatures.

Everyone an Adam

Since Adam was the first created living soul, everyone else came from his loins. Thus, it is accurate to say that everyone is an Adam, or there is an Adam in everyone until that individual becomes born again. If there is an Adam in everyone who is not born again, it means that every inclination of Adam takes residence in them. Their desires, appetites, and choices will not be different from that of the first Adam. It might be in a different degree or propensity, but Adam is Adam, whether he was the first one or the one born in the year 2070, that is if our Lord Jesus Christ [the second and last Adam] delays His second advent.

> *This is the book of the generations of Adam. In the day that God created man, in the likeness of God made He him; male and female created He them; and blessed them, and called their name Adam, in the day which they were created.*
> **Genesis 5:1-2**

Genesis chapter 5 begins by announcing the generations of Adam. This basically was an introduction to the lineage of every human that came out from Adam. This is the record of every "Mere man" that hailed from the living soul, born in the B.C, A.D, the present now or in the future. It is summary of who they are; He made only two genders of them, male, and female, and called the spirit he put in them, Adam (man).

Many Bible versions use different translations for Adam; human beings, the Human race, Mankind, Man, etc. These all mean the same thing, but for the sake of the context of the subject matter of this book let's use the King James Version translation (KJV), Adam.

The man spirit in the male and female genders is still Adam. Thus, everyone who is not born again has an

Adam in him or her, because they still have his nature and spirit. If God called all those who are not yet born-again Adam, what would He call those who are born again by the second and last Adam— Jesus Christ?

Therefore, in the sight of God, there are only two breeds represented—The Adamic Breed and the Breed of Christ Jesus. The Adamic breed represents everyone who is spiritually alienated from God, while the breed of Christ Jesus is everyone that has been reconciled to God through the finished work of Jesus Christ.

The New Creatures; Christ's Image

Who is the image of the invisible God, the firstborn of every creature. **Colossians 1:15**

The New Creatures are not ordinary persons. They are superior to the mere men, the devil, and his cohorts. They are created in the image of Christ Jesus, the second and last Adam. It is fascinating to note how God created man; He didn't just call them forth like He did other creations. He meticulously fashioned man in His image and likeness. This means that Adam was created to be [image] and to function [likeness] like God. But he was made a living soul. He became alive by the breath of God, and he was given full custodian rights to be in charge of the earth, and to name all the animals, but he couldn't give life because he was a living soul. After he fell short of the glory of God, man found himself operating only in the realm of the senses (natural realms), far away from the realm where God can ever be found.

Although he was created in the image and likeness of God, Adam was not filled with the Holy Spirit of God, like the new creature is full of Him after being born again. The reason is that the second and last Adam was made a quickening Spirit (1 Corinthians 15:45), and everyone who is born of Him possess the same Spirit as Christ therefore is made a life-giver (1 Corinthians 6:17),

After God created Adam, He breathed into his nostrils and he came to life, although the breath in Adam was from God's Spirit it was not the person of the Holy Spirit. Thus, we can assuredly say that he only had the breath of God but didn't have the Holy Spirit. The Holy Spirit is a Person; He created Adam, Adam would not have disobeyed God's instructions to him, and moreover, he would have been able to recognize that the devil was in the serpent if he had the Person of the Holy Spirit of God dwelling inside of him.

The case is very different with the new creature, the new creature is created after the image of Christ who is the eternal image of the God head. Hence, the new creature has the Spirit of God, firstly because he was created from the Word of God by His Spirit. Secondly, because he has the Person of the Holy Spirit inside of him, he is now His temple (1 Corinthians 6:19), Adam wasn't the temple of the Holy Spirit.

The new creature is the carrier of God's Spirit in the earth, while Adam is a carrier of God's breath. Thus, everyone who is not yet born again still represents the Adamic lineage, carriers of the breath of God, that makes the human body come alive.

> *Who being the brightness of His glory, the express image of His Person, and upholding all things by the word of His power, when He had by Himself purge our sins, sat down on the right hand of the Majesty on high.* **Hebrews 1:3**

Christ is the image definition of the Godhead and of the new creature because He is the express image of the invisible God, who is Spirit, and the firstborn of the new creatures.

The Fight for Image

There is a fight for image. This is so because image is everything. There is nothing that scares the devil more than believers understanding the image of Whom they have become and also walking in that reality. Thus, the fight for man is the fight for image; a fight between who you are and who you were created to be. The devil tarnished the Adamic image through sin, and infused confusion in the mind of the Adamic race. Now, men declare boldly without shame or fear that they rather get married to the same gender because God created them wrongly. Males believe and insist that they are supposed to be females and females want to be males, all with the claim that they are entrapped in the wrong bodies. How confused can an image be?

The Devil cannot tamper with the image of a new creature because this image is created and founded in Christ, and Christ in God. The image of Christ became possible after Christ defeated Satan and his cohorts in hell. Satan has been defeated in the earth concerning mankind. Jesus won the victory, so Satan is rid of his power—the Adamic dominion power he stole from Adam. And moreover, Christ Himself became the first to be born again with this new creation life.

Christ is the image of God, and the image everyone becomes when they get born again, since the devil knows this, he does all he can to prevent the unbelievers from embracing the gospel of Jesus Christ, which is the only light that has the power to defeat darkness and reveal the true image of the individual.

> *In their case, the god of this world has blinded the minds of the unbelievers, to keep them from seeing the light of the gospel of the glory of Christ, who is the image of God.* **2 Corinthians 4:4 (ESV)**

Image, referenced in this verse of Scripture, is the reason the god of this world have blinded the minds of the Adamic man not to see the light, because as soon as he sees the light of the gospel of Christ, he sees and discovers his true image— that, he is the same image with Christ, born of God in Christ Jesus.

The Word of God [which we preach is the gospel], and it is the mirror of God that reveals the true image of Christ to the Adamic man. Once he decides to look intently into this mirror, everything about him changes and the devil doesn't want that, so he keeps on spitting lies about the gospel in their minds. For the Bible says:

> *But we all, with open faces beholding as in a mirror the glory of the Lord, are changed into the same image from glory to glory, even as by the Spirit of the Lord.* **2 Corinthians 3:18**

The new creature was born with the image of Christ when he was born again. The more he looks into the Word of God (God's mirror) with an open face (consciousness), and continues doing so, the more the revelation of the image he has received begins to unfold and revealed from one level of glory to another level of glory.

Like a newborn baby [Adamic] born with the nature of sin, doesn't become active in committing and experiencing the effects of sin until he begins to indulge in the acts of sin as he grows up (Romans 7:9). So it is with the new creature, born with the image of Christ, doesn't begin to enjoy and reap the full benefits of that nature in him until he begins to grow in the Word of God and respond according to the principles of the kingdom of God.

Christ, the Birthing Place

> *Therefore, if any man be in Christ, he is a new creature, old things are passed away, behold all things are become new.* **2 Corinthians 5:17**

Christ is a place; He is also the Birthing Place for all the new creatures. He is the Eternal Womb of God for "Mere men" to become born again into new creatures. For any creation to be born or birth to happen, a womb is needed for that to happen. In the natural world, the womb is an organ (a place in the human body) in a woman or other female mammal in which an offspring is conceived. So also in the spiritual realm, for the offspring of God to be born again there must be a womb, although not as the natural one; Christ is that Womb where all new creatures are conceived by the Word by the agency of the Holy Spirit into the kingdom of God.

Since Christ is the Birthing Place of the new creature, we can interpret 2 Corinthians 5:17 as thus, *"Therefore if any Adam (Mere man) be in Christ (be conceived and born into Christ) he is a new creature, the former Adamic nature has passed away, see, he is a brand-new being."*

And this new being is born with Eternity in Him, although he still has a body and lives in the Adamic physical world. He is Eternity on two legs, and this Eternity is the Spirit of Christ that birthed him.

According to John 3:6, "That which is born of the flesh is flesh; and that which is born of the Spirit is spirit." This Bible verse reveals to us the fundamental principle of creation, everything was made and created to birth its kind. Mango trees will never produce apples, so also a bird cannot birth a lion. Adam will birth his kind, and Christ will birth His kind as well. So, Adam cannot birth a new creature, and Christ cannot birth a mere man.

> *And so, it is written, the first man Adam was made a living soul; the last Adam was made a quickening Spirit.* **1 Corinthians 15:4**

Because Spirit can only birth spirit, the new creature's spirit is from Christ and it's accurate to say that that spirit in the new creature is Christ. Adam was "made" a living soul and Christ was "made a quickening Spirit." It was the Creator's decision to make them differently, but the second and the last Adam is greater than the first. Every new creature possesses a quickening Spirit within him because that's the Spirit that he was birthed from, and with. The new creature is a life-giving spirit. He has the quickening Spirit within him, therefore nothing should be dead around him. This Bible Translation renders it even better.

The Scriptures tell us,

> *The first man, Adam, became a living person. But the last Adam—that is, Christ—is a life-giving Spirit. What comes first is the natural body, then*

> the spiritual body comes later. Adam, the first man, was made from the dust of the earth, while Christ, the second man, came from heaven. Earthly people are like the earthly man, and the heavenly people are like the heavenly man.
> **I Corinthians 15:45-48 (NLT)**

Either you are an Adam, or you are a Christ on earth. According to this Scripture, there is an earthly man (Adam) whom the earthly people [Mere men] are like unto, and there is the heavenly Spirit (Christ) whom the heavenly people—temporal-earthly-resident [the new creatures] are like as well.

Unpredictable Being

> The wind blows where it wills, and you hear the sound thereof, but cannot tell from where it comes, and where it goes: so is every one that is born of the Spirit. **John 3:8**

The new creature is power on two legs on the earth. An unpredictable being. The Scripture says, that because he is born of the Spirit of Christ he is like the wind. He is not the wind, but like the wind which blows, and you hear the sound thereof but cannot tell from where it comes or where it goes.

The Spirit of Christ in him controls him. He has no more desires of his own, whatever the Lord will have him do that's what he does. He has no more agenda of his own because the life he now lives; he lives by the faith of the Son of God who loved him and gave Himself for him. Although he is assumed to be a normal person everyone used to know in the flesh, he is a new creature, loaded with the power of God. He walks by faith and not by his sensory perceptions, or by the dictates of his physical world. This is Apostle's Paul conclusion about himself as a new creature, and this also applies to everyone who is born again by the Spirit of God.

> *My old self has been crucified with Christ. It is no longer I who live, but Christ lives in me. so, I live in this earthly body by trusting in the Son of God, who loved me and gave Himself for me.*
> **Galatians 2:20 (NLT)**

Some new creatures might be reading this book thinking, I don't recognize any of these in my life. The greatest challenge of many of the new creatures in Christ today is that they have not discovered who they really are in Christ and what Spirit they are made of. This is the greatest deal— to really come to the full knowledge of who you are in Christ Jesus. You are no longer that old Harry, Thompson, Cynthia, or Martha; in heaven there is no more record of your old self, it is the new you that is known. Glory to God!

Chapter Two

Dominion

New Creatures, Wrong Mindset

There are many new creatures who still operate with the mind of the mere man. These are born again, and full of the Holy Spirit but subject themselves to the same mentality or mindset of the mere man. They submit themselves to rules that don't apply to the new creatures, and sadly it is reflected in their speech and actions. Sadly, sometimes it is almost impossible to differentiate these from the mere men. They are not mere men but are those who are born again but are still conformed to this world and its principles, refusing the transformation of the mind that can only happen through the Word of God.

> *You have died with Christ, and he has set you free from the spiritual powers of this world. So why do you keep on following the rules of the world, such as, don't handle! Don't taste! Don't touch!? Such*

> rules are mere human teachings about things that deteriorate as we use them. These rules may seem wise because they require strong devotion, pious self- denial, and severe bodily discipline. But they provide no help in conquering a person's evil desires. **Colossians 2:20-23 (NLT)**

These rules seem wise because they require "strong devotion, pious, self-denial, and severe bodily discipline". These new creatures with the wrong mindset believe genuinely but ignorantly that they are on the right path following these sets of rules. These do's' and don'ts provide no help in conquering a person's evil desire. It is only the Word of God that has the power to conquer the evil desires in a person. Studying, and meditating on the spiritual Truths of the Word of God becomes a genuine struggle for them.

Dominion and Domain

> And God said, let us make, man in our own image, after our likeness: and let them have dominion over the fish of the sea, and over the fowl of the air, and over the cattle, and over all the earth, and over every creeping thing that creeps upon the earth. **Genesis 1:26**

The new creatures have been called to take complete dominion and to live their lives in the earth using the dominion they have received from the Father, through

Jesus Christ. The new creatures are called to take charge in every realm where they are created and to dominate. They are also called to rise above everything that is a hurdle, bondage, or limitation to the mere man.

Since they are now in the kingdom of God, they are called to exercise their dominion from their location in God's kingdom which is in the earth and influence any opposing power.

Their dominion over all things began from the first day they gave their hearts to the Lord. However, many have not come to the full realization of this truth and to the reality of who God has made them to be.

What is Dominion?

Dominion means Sovereignty or control. Also, it is to be in charge of something or rule over it.

Who Was Given Dominion?

If dominion means control, it means something has to be controlled in order for it to be termed as dominion. There is no dominion where there is nothing to dominate. For dominion to be in effect and in operation, there has to be a domain. From the Scriptures, we clearly understand that after the Almighty God, man is the next to have a domain (Earth) because it was given to him by God.

> *The heaven, even the heavens, are the Lord's: but the earth hath he given to the children of men.* **Psalm 115:16**

Angels are wonderful and amazing beings, but they do not have dominion. This is so because they don't have a particular domain allotted to them by God to have sovereignty over. The angels of God dwell in heaven and operate on the earth as they serve those who should inherit salvation (Hebrews 1:14). The devil and his demons were not given dominion, nor was any place found for them any longer (Rev 12.8), but through deception he stole the dominion that was given to Adam (Luke 4:6). Since then, he has created and controlled the "the worldly systems he'd set in place", and operated with the Adamic power he obtained by deception. It is very informative to indicate that everyone who isn't born again, is subject to this stolen dominion. Before it was stolen from him, it was only the Adamic man that had genuine dominion," after God Almighty. This dominion was bequeathed to him by God. And he was to use it to have the rule over all the works of God's hand. Adam was made lord over creation by the God of creation.

> *You have made him to have dominion over the works of your hands; you have put all things under his feet.* **Psalm 8:6**

Four Levels Of Dominion

There are levels or areas where dominion is applicable, and these are:

1. Intellectual Dominion
2. Physical Dominion
3. Spiritual Dominion
4. Supernatural Dominion

It is important to note that the Adamic or the mere man operates in the first three areas of dominion, while the new creature (the image of Christ) is born with the capacity to operate in all levels of dominion.

1. Intellectual Dominion

This level of dominion operates within the realm of the mind, particularly the Adamic mind. With intellectual dominion, the Adamic man can operate, control, and interact directly with his environment using his senses. However, this level of dominion only recognizes what the mind can comprehend and cannot control what is beyond its intellectual reach. It also cannot see far beyond its immediate surroundings.

For example, humans have been able to influence the way their societies are structured.
From the moment a child is born until he grows up, his choice of career and place of residence is often determined by intellectual dominion. The educational

system is designed for the Adamic man to choose a profession within the available framework of their society. They are limited to the options offered by the areas of study available in their country. So, they cannot study to become a microbiologist if there is no opportunity in their society for a profession in that field. The system is structured to dominate the way people live their lives, with their entire existence defined by their profession.

> *Do not conform to the pattern of this world but be transformed by the renewing of your mind. Then you will be able to test and approve what God's will is—His good, pleasing, and perfect will.* **Romans 12:2**

Recognizing the limitations of the Adamic mind, Paul the apostle, inspired by the Holy Spirit, encourages the new creature to work on their mind by daily renewing it with God's Word. Failure to do so means that the new creature would not be able to test and approve what God's will is because their discernment would be limited and based on the level of intellectual dominion. So, Paul urges the new creatures:

> *See to it that no one takes you captive through philosophy and empty deception, according to the tradition of men, according to the elementary principles of the world, rather than according to Christ.* **Colossians 2:8**

Apostle Paul refers to intellectual dominion as elementary, which is what people hold in high esteem and consider the greatest achievement in the world's standard. Men use philosophy and empty deception to captivate unsuspecting mere men in the world. But the new creature must follow the principles of Christ, which provide true freedom. Glory to Jesus forever!

Elementary Principles
Since the spiritual realm is greater than the physical realm, all-natural principles are considered elementary compared to the spiritual. Spiritual dimensions are greater and more sophisticated than any physical principles. It is, therefore, interesting to note that the systems of this world are designed to be elementary, based on what you can touch, taste, smell, see, and hear. These senses became more dominant in the Adamic man after Adam fell short of the glory of God (Romans 3.23). We can further conclude that every elementary principle that governs the systems of the world is based on these five senses.

The Apostle Paul reveals to the new creatures that these principles, which mere men hold in the highest esteem, are nothing but "elementary." The new creature must rise above these five factors that govern the world. The dimensions of Christ are yet to be discovered by the new creatures. We must become aware that there are more realms to operate from in Christ than the elementary principles taught to us by the systems of this world.

2. Physical Dominion

This level of dominion is where mere humans apply their physical strength and abilities to tame or directly control all that is within their domain. They can use their strength forcefully or tactically to exert control over other humans and terrestrial animals. However, it is essential to recognize that this level of dominion is limited in that it can only function within the earthly realm and is primarily exerted on terrestrial animals. For example, animals are often taken from their natural habitats and confined by the will and strength of humans. Human beings are imprisoned and incarcerated, where their freedom of movement is restricted and constrained by others. An example from the Bible that illustrates the consequences of physical restraint is found in the book of Matthew:

> *Settle matters quickly with your adversary who is taking you to court. Do it while you are still together on the way, or your adversary may hand you over to the judge, and the judge may hand you over to the officer, and you may be thrown into prison.* **Matthew 5:25 (NIV)**

This verse explains how physical dominion operates within the context of human interactions and the judicial system. It demonstrates how restrictions not of one's choosing can be imposed on individuals by others who have been given physical dominion and the authority to do so, often through legal and constitutional means. Historical examples such as slavery were based on this realm of dominion, where slave masters, often self-proclaimed explorers, imposed their physical dominance using weapons and chains to transport people forcibly from their homes to foreign lands.

3. Spiritual Dominion

The verse, "For as the body without the spirit is dead, so faith without works is dead" (James 2:26) emphasizes the connection between the physical body and the spirit. The Adamic man was created as a spirit, possessing a soul, and dwelling in a body. Prior to the entrance of sin into the world, Adam's spirit was spiritually aware and in communion with God. However, following his rebellion against God, he became a mere man, and the acute awareness of his spirit towards God waned, leading to his fall from God's glory.

Before the fall, Adam was capable of connecting and communing with God on a one-on-one level. This interaction likely occurred in the realm of the spirit, as "God is Spirit, and no flesh can see God and live" (Exodus 33:20). During this time, his spirit held greater dominance over his senses, and he did not need to exert extraordinary efforts to maintain this connection with God. However, after his fall, his spiritual awareness waned, and the dominance of his senses increased, making it necessary for him to exert extra effort to reconnect with God.

Spiritual dominion can be utilized for both good and evil purposes, depending on the spiritual influence operating within an individual. In the case of the new creature, their spirit is influenced by the Holy Spirit, allowing them to use spiritual dominion wisely for their own benefit and the benefit of others. Conversely, the spirits of mere humans can be influenced by wicked demonic forces that take possession of them. Through such demonic possession, individuals exert spiritual dominance to control, influence, or dominate others. It is common to find individuals delving into occult practices, sorcery, the New Age, astral and magical dimensions, consulting with witches and warlocks, and engaging with various mediums that work with evil and wicked spirits to cast demonic spells to manipulate and control people.

An example of this malevolent spiritual dominance is found in **Acts 8:9-11**:

> *But there was a certain man, called Simon, who formerly practiced sorcery in the same city and amazed the people of Samaria, claiming that he was someone great. They all gave heed to him, from the least to the greatest, saying, 'This man is the great power of God.' To him they had regard because, for a long time, he had bewitched them with his sorceries.*

Ignorantly, the people regarded this man as having the great power of God. Through sorcery, he succeeded in bewitching the entire city of Samaria, exerting spiritual dominance over the people without their realization. The people were so bewitched that they could no longer distinguish the power of God from that of a sorcerer. This control and manipulation were possible because the people living in Samaria at that time were still spiritually dead to God and His Word.

Supernatural Dominion & Supernatural Intervention
In Judges chapter 15, from verses fourteen to fifteen, we find the story of how Samson, a judge of Israel at that time, subdued a thousand Philistines using nothing but the jawbone of a donkey. In this case, it was the supernatural power of God, specifically the Spirit of might, that came upon Samson and enabled him to exert physical dominance over a thousand trained Philistine soldiers (Judges 15:16).

> *He guards the feet of His saints, but the wicked shall be silent in darkness. For by strength shall no man prevail.* **1 Samuel 2:9**

The supernatural interventions of God by His Spirit consistently render all levels of Adamic dominion ineffective. Although dominion was initially given to humankind, God expects individuals to give Him all the glory and credit for their dominion, as it rightfully belongs to Him. God also does not want people to take pride in their natural strength and physical abilities. In this regard, the Word of the Lord to Zerubbabel is a valuable reference:

> *This is the word of the Lord to Zerubbabel: 'Not by might nor by power, but by My Spirit,' says the Lord of hosts.* **Zechariah 4:6**

This verse underscores that power and dominion belong to God, and anyone granted the opportunity to exercise any level of power or dominion should honor and give glory to the One to whom all power belongs.

> *Once God has spoken; twice have I heard this: that power belongs to* God. **Psalms 62:11 (ESV)**

An instance from the early church found in Acts 12:3-19 involves the arrest of the apostle Peter by Herod, who had previously executed James by the sword. Peter was imprisoned, and sixteen soldiers were ordered to guard him. His execution was scheduled after the celebration of Easter. However, the church decided to pray earnestly until the Lord sent supernatural intervention. Supernatural intervention from the Lord is consistently more powerful than physical dominion. In this case, Peter was confined and couldn't do much but sleep, with no record of him praying or worshiping God while in prison. The church's earnest and heartfelt prayers were necessary for his release. This example demonstrates that, according to the order and hierarchy within the kingdom of God, it is not only permitted but also possible for the church or a group of believers to intercede in situations involving physical dominion through earnest and heartfelt prayers.

In a similar scenario, the case of Paul and Silas in Acts 16:16- 40 involved their arrest after confronting a situation where a man was exploiting a girl who was possessed by familiar spirits for profit through fortune-telling. When Paul casts out the demon from the girl, her owners decide to involve the authorities, leading to the arrest of Paul and Silas. They were physically chained and held in the innermost part of the prison. However, they did not passively wait for others to determine their fate; instead, they began to sing hymns, pray, and praise God. The supernatural intervention was sent by the Lord, suspending every form of physical dominion exerted upon them.

The Gospel is the Power of God
The Gospel of our Lord and Savior, Jesus Christ, is the power of God unto salvation and freedom from every shape, form, kind, and type of evil spiritual dominion. Once the city of Samaria heard and accepted the gospel, the scales of diabolic spiritual dominion fell from their eyes, including Simon, the sorcerer. A man capable of controlling an entire city with sorcery is no small practitioner in the art of sorcery. He became born again, was baptized, and continued with Philip, marveling at the miracles and signs performed through the hands of Philip. He marveled at these miracles and signs because

what he encountered through the ministry of the Holy Spirit in Philip surpassed any power of sorcery.

> But when they believed Philip, preaching the things concerning the kingdom of God and the name of Jesus Christ, they were baptized, both men and women. Then Simon himself believed also, and when he was baptized, he continued with Philip, and marveled, beholding the miracles and signs which were done. **Acts 8:12-13**

The new creature has been given the power of God unto salvation and total freedom (The Gospel), and we must engage our nations and cities, destroying and breaking the chains and bondages of every diabolic spiritual dominion that has held people down for too long. It is our duty and responsibility. We owe everyone in our world this. Glory to God forever!

4. Supernatural Dominion

Supernatural dominion is the level of dominion that our Lord Jesus Christ has made possible for the new creature to operate in. This level of dominion eludes the mere man because his spirit is not regenerated. He cannot attain or walk in this realm unless he becomes born again.

Supernatural dominion is the ability to have influence in heavenly matters concerning the kingdom on earth, to exert influence on earth and in hell while still on earth. The scope of this level of dominion covers all of creation.

It is recognized and approved by heaven, obeyed on earth, and feared in hell.

Let's Go Deeper
According to Genesis 1:26, the Adamic man was given dominion "over" the fish in the sea, the fowl of the air, and everything living that moved upon the earth. However, new creatures were given dominion power and authority to "tread or trample" upon serpents and scorpions and over all the power of the enemy.

The dictionary definition of the word "over" means to be higher in rank than, to have preference and control. While the words "tread or trample" mean to stamp or walk roughly with the intention to crush or hurt. Synonyms for "tread" include override, revoke, annul, veto, trample, nullify, quash, cancel, and defeat.

Adam was higher in rank than all creation because he was preferred by God to be so, and he was given the right to express control as the god over the systems of the earth.

Dominion and Power

Adam had dominion given to him by God, but he was not given power. He was not given power because he had dominion. And since power is not needed where there is no threat to your well-being. Dominion was enough for Adam to govern the earth successfully because when

God gave him the right to control others, all creation heard that command.

Dominion means control and Power means inherent ability or capacity to direct or influence the behavior of others or the course of events. The new creature received power when he was filled with the Holy Ghost. He also received dominion and power(authority) to crush, all the power of the enemy. He'd been given the right to exert judgment.

> Do you know that we will judge angels? How much more the things in this life! **1 Corinthians 6:3**

Imagine this amazing revelation to the new creature, that if the new creature would judge angels in the life that is to come, what about judging the things on the earth in this life now?

When God spoke to Adam, the enemy was not a concern (serpent, the devil), because Adam was preferred, higher in rank, and lord over all things. In fact, Adam was the main threat and enemy to the serpent but wasn't aware of this. Therefore, God didn't instruct Adam or give him power over the enemy, because Adam didn't need power for anything, as long as he had dominion. As long as he controlled his realm the devil wasn't a threat.

The Fear and Dread of Adam

The same instructions and commands God gave to Adam after creation were the same ones He gave to Noah after the flood:

> *The fear of you and the dread of you shall be upon every beast of the earth, and upon every bird in the heavens, upon everything that creeps on the ground and all the fish of the sea. Into your hand they are delivered.* **Genesis 9:2**

God put the fear and dread of Adam and Noah (Mankind) on everything in the realms of the earth. When animals see or encounter mankind, their first response or reaction is fear and dread of him, because of his right of dominion. Man is not necessarily the biggest in size naturally, nor is he physically or naturally the fastest, but in dominion he is the greatest.

> *You have given him dominion over the works of your hands; you have put all things under his feet, all sheep, and oxen, and also the beasts of the field, the birds of the heavens, and the fish of the sea, whatever passes along the seas.* **Psalm 8:6-8**

Our Lord Jesus brought the new creature a better deal. He gave us dominion power (authority) over serpents and scorpions and over all the power of the enemy. To this end, Jesus indicates to the new creature that there is an enemy, but that the enemy is not a match for the new creature.

The Fear and Dread of the New Creature

Just as God put the fear and dread of Adam on all animals, birds, and fishes, the fear and the dread of the new creature is put on the enemy and his cohorts by Jesus Christ; because of the name of Jesus Christ that is mentioned on every new creature, the devil and his demons naturally fear and dread the new creature. But how many new creatures know and recognize this truth?

The statement, "Over every creeping thing that creeps upon the earth", was the last to be mentioned because they were not a threat. But when Jesus was talking to His disciples, serpents and scorpions were the first to be mentioned, because now they are a threat when allowed to have their way—although the fear and dread of the new creature has been put upon them.

> *Behold, I give you power to tread on serpents and scorpions, and over all the power of the enemy, and nothing shall by any means hurt you.* **Luke 10:19**

> *And these signs shall follow them that believe; in my name shall they cast out devils, they shall speak with new tongues; they shall take up serpents; and if they drink any deadly thing, it*

> *shall not hurt them; they shall lay hands on the sick and they shall recover.* **Mark 16:17-18**

Glory to God! He has given awesome privilege and power to the new creatures by our Lord and Savior Jesus Christ.

When Adam was created, there was no man representative in heaven. It was God the Father, the Word, and the Holy Spirit. But now, there is a representative of man in heaven, and He is the very definition and embodiment of power and dominion—Jesus Christ is His Name. Hallelujah!

The lesser is blessed by the greater (Hebrews 7:7), and since the new creature possesses the nature of God (Zoe), he is greater than the Adamic man, thus he has been given power over all in the Adamic realms and systems. The Man- Representative rules over all and the new creature is in Him, ruling over all from the Highest of High. Glory to God!

> *Far above all principality, and power, and might, and dominion, and every name that is named, not only in this world but that which is to come.* **Ephesians 1:21**

Jesus is the dominion power of the new creature because we are joined with Him (1 Corinthians 6:17). Power can only be inherent, meaning an ability, or capacity that self-exits permanently or is built in someone. Power can also be vested in someone in whom it is or was not inherent.

That's what happened to every new creature when they were born again. We all received the inherent ability of God—The Holy Ghost.

> *And you shall receive power, after that the Holy Ghost is come upon you, and you shall be witnesses unto me both in Jerusalem, in Judea, in Samaria and unto the utmost part of the earth.* **Acts 1:8**

Because the new creature has inherent power in him (The Holy Ghost), he is set far above all principality, power, might, dominion, and every name that is named, not only in this world but in that which is to come.

> *Beloved, now are we the sons of God, and it doth not yet appear what we shall be: but we know that, when He shall appear, we shall be like Him, for we shall see Him as He is.* **1 John 3:2**

Therefore, because of where Christ has elevated him, the supernatural dominion given to the new creature exceeds the realm and frame of time. it extends to the world and ages to come, because of the Man Jesus, our Man-Representative in Heaven.

Daniel Saw It:
The forever dominion power and glory of Jesus Christ were revealed to the prophet Daniel in the Old Testament, even before there was any physical Person named Jesus Christ.

> *And to Him was given dominion and glory and a kingdom, that all peoples, nations, and languages should serve Him: His dominion is an everlasting dominion, which shall not pass away, and His kingdom, one that shall not be destroyed.* **Daniel 7:14**

And the Apostle Peter saw it as well:

> *To Him be glory, and dominion forever and ever. Amen.* **1 Peter 5:11**

Glory be to Jesus Christ forever and ever!

Dominion to Tame

Dominion is all about hierarchical positioning. Everyone and everything under the preferred or chosen dominant one bows and submits to him. The dominant one is given the right and ability to tame others under him.

What Does Tame Mean?
To tame means to domesticate, break, train, master, subdue, enslave, docile. This is the process of exerting dominion over humans or animals to bring them into conformity of the desires or expectations of the tamer. For example, a human can be enslaved so long that they conform to whatever their master demands and desires. Likewise, animals, taken from the wild can become domesticated through the process of taming.

> *For every kind of beast and bird, or reptile and sea creature, can be tamed, and has been tamed by mankind.* **James 3:7**

If the Adamic man can tame and has tamed all creatures in his realm with intellectual, physical, and spiritual. Then the new creature who is made superior to the Adamic man is even more powerful, thus everything under him can be tamed and has been tamed for him by Jesus Christ. The Man Jesus has tamed the devil, and his demons and every circumstance. They were once wild on the earth, running rampant after stealing the dominion of Adam to control his realm. But now they have all been tamed by Jesus Christ who has disarmed all the powers of the devil and his cohorts when he made a public spectacle in hell and led captivity captive.

> *And having disarmed the spiritual rulers and authorities. He shamed them publicly by His victory over them on the cross.* **Colossians 2:15 (NLT)**

He defeated them all, and gave the power to tame or domesticate to this new creature.

> *Therefore, it is said, that when He ascended on high, He led captivity captive [he led a train of vanquished foes] and He bestowed gifts on men. [But He ascended?] Now what can this, He ascended, mean but that He had previously descended from [the heights of] heaven into*

> *[the depths], the lower parts of the earth? He who descended is the [very] same as He Who also ascended high above all the heavens, that He [His presence] might fill all things [the whole universe, from the lowest to the highest]. -* **Ephesians 4:8-9 (AMP)**

Once upon a time in the earth, the devil and the fallen angels used to be powerful and ran rampage in the world. He had the freedom to do what he liked and wanted, only God was stronger than him. He succeeded in leeching humanity as he so desired until the Man Jesus came on the scene. Now, "all" power in heaven, on earth, and beneath the earth has been given to Jesus Christ, and Jesus Christ gave it to his new creatures. Hallelujah!

The Name of Jesus Christ has Tamed all things! In, with and by the Name of Jesus, the new creature has been given the authority to domesticate the devil and his cohorts.

> *For by Him, all things were created, in heaven, and on earth, visible and invisible, whether thrones, dominions, rulers or authorities—all things were created through Him and for Him. -* **Colossians 1:16**

> *Who, although being essentially one with God and in the form of God [possessing the fullness of the attributes which make God God], did not think this equality with God was a thing to be*

eagerly grasped or retained. But stripped Himself [of all privileges and rightful dignity], so as to assume the guise of a servant (slave), in that He became like men and was born a human being. And after He had appeared in human form, He abased and humbled Himself [still further] and carried His obedience to the extreme of death, even the death of the cross! Therefore [because He stopped so low] God has highly exalted Him and has freely bestowed on Him the name that is above every name, that in (at) the name of Jesus every knee should (must) bow, in heaven and on earth and under the earth, and every tongue [frankly and openly] confess and acknowledge that Jesus Christ is Lord, to the glory of God the Father. **Philippians 2:6-11 (AMP)**

Imagine you as a new creature, taking "full advantage" of the name of Jesus. The name Jesus was given to Jesus after all that He subjected Himself to go through for all humanity— He didn't have to do it, but He made a choice to do it and on how He would do it. He stripped himself of His God attributes, allowed Himself to be found in human form, and became obedient to death. And because of all of this He did and has done, God highly exalted His Name.

We have a Name, a Name that is the greatest Name ever known in Heaven, on Earth, and in Hell.

And I heard every creature in Heaven, and on earth, and under the Earth, and in the sea, and all that is in them saying: To Him who sits on the throne, and unto the Lamb, be praise and honor and glory and power forever and ever.
Revelation 5:13

Glory be to God forever for the wonderful gift of the Name of Jesus Christ.

Chapter Three

Seeds

Except for God, who is Life Himself, all forms of life come in the forms of seeds—the natural and the spiritual seed. Encapsulated in a seed is the DNA and the structure for life. Everything that is a being, animal or plant will become what is stored in the seed. Thus, if the right seed get planted in the right soil or environment, the right harvest is inevitable. As mentioned in the previous chapter, every seed eventually produces its kind as long as that seed is not tampered with. Natural bringing forth the natural and the spiritual birthing the spiritual.

The Natural Seed

Everything God created on earth came out from the earth. He didn't have to import anything from heaven, He used what was present in the earth, calling those things that be not as though they were. And the earth responded as thus, firstly yielding the plants and trees with their seeds in their kind and then the animals coming out from the ground in their kinds because God spoke it to be so.

> *This is the account of God's creation of plants, trees, and their seeds in their kind, the fishes and all sea monsters, birds and animals in their kinds:So, God said, "Let the earth sprout [tender] vegetation, plants yielding seed, and fruit trees bearing fruit according to (limited to, consistent with) their kind, whose seed is in them upon the earth"; and it was so. The earth sprouted and abundantly produced vegetation, plant yielding seed according to their kind, and trees bearing fruit with seed in them, according to their kind; and God saw that it was good and He affirmed and sustained it.* **Genesis 1:11-12 (AMP)**
>
> *God created the great sea monsters and every living creature that moves, with which the waters swarmed according to their kind, and every winged bird according to its kind; and God saw that it was good and He affirmed and sustained it. And God blessed them, saying, 'Be fruitful, multiply, and fill the waters in the seas, and let the birds multiply on the earth'.* **Genesis 1:21-22 (Amp)**
>
> *Then God said, 'Let the earth bring forth living creatures according to (limited to, consistent*

> with) their kind: livestock, crawling things, and wild animals of the earth according to their kinds"; and it was so [because He had spoken them into creation] So God made the wild animals of the earth according to their kind, and the cattle according to their kind, and everything that creeps and crawls in the earth according to its kind; and God saw that it was good (pleasing, useful) and He affirmed and sustained it. **Genesis 1:24-25 (Amp)**

In the natural world, stored in a single seed is the mystery of multiplication, that no man has been able to unravel. What makes one single seed produce many after some time? Why does it not remain as one seed in the ground? Concerning His death and burial, and also teaching His disciples a very important principle, Jesus reveals that the principles of multiplication can only happen if the seed is willing first to disengage itself and is ready to die, it abides by itself. In essence, when the seed gets buried into the earth and submits to the process of germination and the law of growth, the multiplication codes within the seed are activated. There must be a harvest eventually, and this harvest will not be one seed, but many of the same kind that was buried inside the ground.

> Very truly I tell you, unless a kernel of wheat falls to the ground and dies, it remains only a single seed. But if it dies, it produces many seeds. **John 12:24 (NIV)**

Thus, the law of multiplication responds to the death of a single seed. But that seed must first come in contact with the right environment. This is also a spiritual principle. According to Scriptures, there is no seed, time, and harvest in Heaven (Genesis 8:22). Earth is the only realm that experiences seed sowing and harvest, because in Heaven, things are not planted, they are and become by the spoken word of God. Thus, Heaven was not the right environment for God to plant His Seed (Jesus Christ). Christ Jesus had to come to earth and die on earth because earth is where seeds are planted, even though the Lamb was slain before the foundation of the world (Revelation 13:8). He was planted (Buried) in the belly of the earth and after three days, He germinated (rose up again) to produce billions of seeds for the Father who is the owner of the Seed, and also the vineyard.

Spiritual Seed

> *By the word of the Lord the heavens were made, their starry host by the breath of his mouth.*
> **Psalm 33:6 (NIV)**

In the realm of the spirit, the other form of seeds are words. Words are seeds, and by these seeds, God created all things. This seed is incorruptible, eternal, and forever durable. This seed is the only seed that can operate or function both in Heaven and on Earth, producing fruits. The natural seed is very particular to the Earth realm and it has no chance in Heaven. In reality, it is the spiritual seed that created the natural seed. Jesus is the Word of God by Whom He made all things;

> *Now this is the meaning of the parable: the seed is the Word of God.* **Luke 8:11**

> *In the beginning was the Word and the Word was with God and the Word was God.* **John 1:1**

> *And He was clothed with a clothing dipped in blood: and His name is called the Word of God.* **Revelation 19:13**

The Word is the Seed, and the Seed is the Word, and Jesus Christ is the Word of God. He is God's Seed by Whom all new creatures are born and created. After His death, burial, and resurrection more than two thousand years ago. He is still producing seeds and fruits like Himself, of the same kind. The new creatures are born of the Word. Think about it, as a new creature, you are bloodline now is a spiritual one, you are born from the Word Himself. Seeds don't struggle to produce their kind, and after producing their kind, their kind doesn't struggle to produce as well because they are made of the same stock. New creatures have the same life as Jesus has. He is the Vine, and we are the branches (John 15). The same life that goes through the vine is the same life that goes through the branches as well. That's the reason the new creature cannot be separated from what he was made from. He is what he was born again from—the Word of God.

> *For you have been born again [that is, reborn from above, spiritually transformed, renewed, and set apart for His purpose] not of seed which is perishable but [from that which is] imperishable and immortal, and that is through the living and everlasting word of God. For all flesh is like grass, and all its glory like the flower of grass. The grass withers and the flower falls off. But the word of the Lord endures forever. And this is the Word [the good news of salvation which was preached to you].* **1 Peter 1:23-25 (Amp)**

This Scripture explains that the new creature is born again from a seed that is not perishable, not liable to decay because its source is from the Seed that came from above. And he is made from that Seed he endures forever, because he is born with eternity. And then there was a comparison made between the new creature and the mere man. All Adamic flesh is like grass and its glory is like the flower of grass. This means that the mere man is born into the frame of time and quickly that time fades away because his seed is from Adam. While the new creature was born with eternity, and eternity cannot be defined by time.

Eternity in Their Heart

The dictionary defines Eternity as a state to which time has no application, timelessness. Unending perpetuity, where time doesn't exist. In line with the Word of God, I consider the dictionary's definition of eternity very limited. You cannot define eternity from the realm of time. Since the Adamic mind hasn't experienced eternity, the definitions presented are based on the assumption that Eternity is the direct opposite of time. There is more about eternity than just it's timelessness. One of these aspects is that time is an interruption in Eternity. Eternity is the realm of the new creatures, because they are born with and in it. Time is not a threat or factor to what they decide to do and accomplish.

Man was created to live forever but was placed in a body that is conditioned to the elements within the frame of time, and he was positioned in the frame of time to rule in the earth as God's regent. He was ordained to function in the capacity of a creator like his Creator. Nothing was to be a hindrance unto him.

God created everything first and planted a garden before creating Adam. He placed man in that Garden of Eden to enjoy and take care of all the Works of His hands. But the presence of sin brought in limitations in the life of mankind that only the second and last Adam—Christ Jesus, has the power to end. He has brought all limitations to an end, except for the last enemy—death (already defeated), shall soon be destroyed (1 Corinthians 15:26). Christ has power over death; death became subject to His name after He died and conquered sin and the grave. The destruction of death is what is left to be done. A frame of eternity when no one or nothing experiences death in the New Heaven and new Earth. Death is a spiritual enemy that was unleashed into the realms of man. Although a wicked spirit, it has the power to affect every natural thing in the world of humans and bring their function within the "frame of time to a halt.

> *He has made everything beautiful in his time: also he has put eternity in men's hearts, so that no man can find out the work the God makes from the beginning to the end.* **Ecclesiastes 3:11**

Why Eternity?

If God hath set or put eternity in the hearts of men, why does time still determine what they do? How is it that everything that man does is done within the confines of time? Time subdues his age, plans, activities, and his ability to function in endless perpetuity on the earth within the frame of time.

Ecclesiastes 3:11 tells us that God has set eternity in the hearts of men, so that no man is able to find us His work from beginning to the end. Why would God do that to the one He gave dominion over all the works of His hands (Psalm 8;6)? Putting eternity in their heart would have been the avenue by which man is able to discover or find out His work. He placed eternity in his heart and then put a limitation on that eternity? That doesn't sound like the God who gives all things liberally and upbraid not (James 1:5).

Before we proceed further, the Holy Spirit gave me a definition of "Eternity in their hearts." **Eternity in the heart of men means an endless world of resources beyond the frame of time and any human scope of comprehension.**

Man has received an endless world of resources that is beyond the frame of what time can dictate or hinder, but unfortunately, man is still very limited in all that he does. This man that is limited, controlled, and hindered by time is the Adamic man or the Mere man. Although he has eternity set in his heart, he cannot do much concerning the work that God is doing from the beginning to the end. This is so because he is separated from God due to sin. He is not in Christ Jesus, thus he can't have God dwell in him. He is far away from his creator and God. He is spiritually dead to God and His works. Due to sin, this Adamic man cannot find out God and His works even if he tries. He must accept and embrace Christ first, and through Christ, he becomes a new creature, possessing the ability and capacity to know God and the works He has done from the beginning to the end.

Chapter Four

The new "gods" on earth

The "gods"

Only gods create, man is a god, so he can create. He is a god because God made him so, he was created in the image and likeness of God. If a lion cannot give birth to a bird, God can only birth gods. Only gods have dominion to rule a domain, the Adamic man was given dominion of the realms of time. From the first day he opened his eyes in the frame of time, man was and still is a god.

The "god" of This World

> *In whom the god of this age has blinded the minds of them who believe not, lest the light of the glorious gospel of Christ, who is the image of God, should shine unto them.* **2 Corinthians 4:4**

In the Scriptures, we understand that the first "god" of this world was Lucifer, who became the Devil (see

Isaiah 14:13-15; Ezekiel 28:13). When he fell, he was cast out and he lost his domain and power. God then created Adam, to rule in the earth domain and to have dominion. So, we can say that the original god of this recreated Earth and world was Adam. He was the god of this world because God gave him dominion and made all things subject to him and his authority. The earth was his home and he was supposed to create a world (a spiritual system of governance that would affect all the natural systems) within the earth given to him. He was tempted, tricked and his dominion stolen from him by the devil (Luke 4:6). From the time Adam handed over the dominion to the devil, the devil became "the god of this age. 'Some Bible translations use the word 'world' instead of 'age.' Satan is the god of this world and age because this age or dispensation is within the frame of time and he cannot rule beyond the lease God placed on the age.

So, Satan the god of this world succeeded in blinding the minds of Mere Men. So that the glorious gospel of Christ, who is the image of God, should shine on them.

I know we have already discussed this subject in Chapter One, but I would like to put more emphasis on this because once the new creature realizes his real image and begins to walk therein fully, there is nothing he cannot achieve in this world. He walks victoriously every single day of his life on this earth. Christ Jesus is the image of God revealed; whoever accepts Christ and His gospel becomes a new creature, and this new creature is birthed in the image of God, because of His supplanted nature in him. The devil knows that the acceptance of the gospel of Christ by any mere man is the exposure of his lies, so he does everything in his reach to blind their minds. All mere men are under the hold of the devil, doesn't matter who they are, as long as they have not accepted the glorious gospel of Christ, the devil has power over them. But, when you accept Christ and His glorious gospel, you break free from the dominion of the god of this world. You now have authority in the name of Jesus Christ over him and his kingdom.

> *The 'gods' know nothing, they understand nothing. They walk in darkness; all the foundations of the earth are shaken. "I said, you are gods, you are all the sons of the Most High. But you will die like mere mortals; you will fall like every other ruler."* **Psalm 82:5-7 (NIV)**

They are gods, yet they know nothing. They were created as gods, yet they understand nothing and in darkness, they wallow because the god of this world has blinded their minds. Because of sin they now die like mere men. The utmost of God's creation created in His image and likeness is now considered as a mere mortal because he has corrupted his nature with sin. Only gods are given dominion to rule and also a domain to rule over. His dominion he gave to another, who now run rampage in the world wrecking-havoc.

The Glorious Gospel

It is the duty and ministry of every new creature, everyone born again to showcase this glorious gospel. The only gospel that can free mere men is the gospel of our Lord and Savior Jesus Christ. The only remedy to the blindness of mere men's mind is the gospel, the devil is afraid and scared of the gospel, because that's the only truth that can expose his lies, and bring to an end his reign over the lives of mortal men.

> *The god of this age has blinded the minds of unbelievers, so that they cannot see the light of the gospel that displays the glory of Christ, who is the image of God.* **2 Corinthians 4:4 (NIV)**

So, we must aggressively preach and enforce this glorious gospel in all the worlds of mere men. Some will fight and kick against it because although their optical eyes are wide open, their minds are blinded. The gospel displays the glory of Christ, and by going to every man's world, we introduce or display this glory for them to see who they are in God through Christ.

Apostle Paul writing to the church at Corinth and all the believers of Christ, explains explicitly the importance of this gospel that is so glorious the devil fears it.

> *But even if our gospel is [in some sense] hidden [behind a veil], it is hidden [only] to those who are perishing; among them the god of this world*

> *[Satan] has blinded the minds of the unbelieving to prevent them from seeing the illuminating light of the gospel of the glory of Christ, who is the image of God. For we do not preach ourselves, but Jesus Christ as Lord, and ourselves [merely] as your bond servants for Jesus' sake. For God who said, "Let light shine out of darkness," is the One who has shone in our hearts to give us the Light of the knowledge of the glory and majesty of God [clearly revealed in the face of Christ.* **2 Corinthians 4:4- 6 (AMP)**

Every time we preach the gospel of Christ, we are commanding light out of darkness, we are saying, "Let light shine out of darkness." As long as they are mere men, they represent the kingdom of darkness and they wallow in darkness, and because the glorious gospel of Jesus Christ is the Only Light that can illuminate the life of mere men, in the reality of it, 'creation' occurs when we preach this gospel. Like God stepped into the earth in Genesis 1, when it was all dark and void, and commanded light to shine out of such condition. We are to command light out of the darkness. No unbeliever is beyond the reach of salvation, and the light of the glorious gospel of Christ. Doesn't matter how dirty we consider their lifestyles to be or how evil they may have become," Light can come out of that darkness." And this light is the glorious gospel of Jesus Christ.

Creators with Words

Many underestimate the power of the Word of God. This is because it has not become a revelation to the hearts of them even in the body of Christ today. The Word of God is more powerful than anyone can imagine. It is far greater than any how we could imagine it to be. Consider the spoken word of God, and how God used His words from the book of Genesis through to the book of Revelation, where He spoke the world into existence. By faith we understand that the worlds were framed by word of God (Hebrews 11:3). And by the Word of God were the Heavens made... He spoke it and it was done; He commanded and it stood firm (Psalm 33:6-9). When He was creating in Genesis chapter 1, whatever God said happened exactly how He called it. Bear in mind that His Words was His Son "through whom also He made the worlds" (Hebrews 1:2). "For in Him (Christ) were all things created..." (Colossians 1:16). And "All things were made through Him; and without Him was not anything made that has been made" (John 1:3). All these God created using His Seed, the Seed who is the Word, and the Word who is His Son—Jesus Christ the Word made flesh.

Consider also how powerful the written word of God is. In the days of Jesus, it was just the Old Testament books that were available. They didn't have the complete Bible like we have it today. Yet, it was so powerful that by quoting it Jesus resisted the devil (Matthew 4). Every

Word of God is powerful regardless written or spoken, the new creature must engage the Word because that's the material needed for creation.

Jesus Himself taught us also in the Scriptures that He is upholding all things by the word of His power (Hebrews 1:3). Imagine the tremendous amount of power it takes to sustain the entire universe. Because in Him all things consist (Colossians 1:17). By His spoken word, He calmed the sea, healed the lepers, raised Lazarus and others from the dead, fed the five and four thousand hungry men women, and children (excluded), with bread and fishes.

Because He is the Word, and also the Seed (Genesis 3:15) by which God created all things. And we are also complete in Him (Colossians 2:10). We can do what He did by using Words to create. Because our physical bodies are still in the frame of time, we create in time from Eternity (we are born in and with it). And from eternity where we are in Christ Jesus, we change the course of events that happen in time. Time cannot change or affect time, nor can it affect eternity. Rather, Eternity affects and changes Time. In Mark 11:12-24, Jesus (eternity) spoke to a fig tree (that's in the realm of time) and the fig tree obeyed. Although it was not the natural season for figs, all things must obey and produce for Him in and out of their seasons. His season is the right season for all creation.

We can only do what God the Father has done from the book of Genesis through to Revelation, and also what Christ Jesus did whilst He was on earth. Speak creation into existence using words, the new creatures must consciously begin to be aware of the power of Words, creating whatever they desire, because they are creators like their Christ and Heavenly Father.

Jesus the God-Man

Our Lord and Savior Jesus came into the earth, with the full understanding of who He is. He is Eternity, the One by whom all things in heaven, earth, and in the seas were made. He had an exchange with the religious leaders of His day. So severe was this exchange that they picked up stones to stone Him because He declared to them that He is the Son of God.

> *Once again, the people picked up stones to kill him. Jesus said, "At my Father's direction I have done many good works. For which one are you going to stone me?"* **John 10:31-32**

The worst of mere men are the religious ones. These mere men took up stones to stone the Creator of the Universe because in their mind He was equating Himself with God—which He is. Their mortal and religious minds couldn't fathom how someone, who they believed looked like them would be God—someone who grew up among them, ate the same food as them, and lived in the same environment as them. He shows up later in His adult years with twelve disciples and crowds following Him around, and He is claiming to be God. The same God that was described in their Torah, the One who brought their ancestors from Egypt through the Red Sea. The same God they built the Temple in Jerusalem to worship. And before them is "a Man" claiming to be that same God. They couldn't come to terms with such a bold statement, and they were ready to defend their ignorance. So, they picked up stones to mete out judgment, for their God. They responded to Him; "We're stoning you not for any good work, but for blasphemy! You, a mere man, claim to be God (John 10:33).

Mere men are spiritually ignorant, concerning the works of God they walk in darkness, yet they are gods. They are quick to oppose the revelation of others who have discovered their position in God. The response of Jesus kept them all silent:

> *Jesus replied, "it is written in your own Scriptures that God said to certain leaders of the people, ' I say, you are gods! And you know that the Scripture cannot be altered. So if those people who received God's message were called 'gods'. Why do you call it blasphemy when I say, 'I am the Son of God? After all, the Father set me apart and sent me into the world'.* **John 10:34-36**

They were ignorant of what the Scripture said about them. They only understood that men were 'mere' because of Adam's transgression, but they failed to realize that the mere man was made a god from the very beginning.

The New "gods" On Earth

Whoever possesses the authority is the lord over the rest. Through Christ, the new creatures are the only ones the devil obeys, because of the name of Jesus. The believer of Christ who knows who he is and what's been accorded him by and in Christ is the one that can send chills down the spine of the devil and his cohorts. We have been given the mandate to expand our kingdom—the kingdom of God everywhere we are. And thus exposing the lies of the devil, curing men of their spiritual blindness, and putting every opposing force against our kingdom in their respective places.

The new creatures are gods in the earth and not of the world. Jesus prayed to the Father for the new creatures,

> *"I have given them Your word and the world has hated them; for they are not of the world, just as I am not of the world."* **John 17:14**

He understands that the new creatures are in the earth but had to deal with an ungodly worldly system built up by Satan. Although their activities and physical lives may be in the realms of this world that controls mere men, they are not from there.

Born from Above

The gods of the earth are born from above. They may look like mere men on the outside, but don't be fooled by their appearances, there is nothing normal about them. They have been given power and authority to do business on behalf of the kingdom they represent. Their words are powerful bringing about what they declare. These new creatures are the most dangerous beings in existence because the name of their God is mentioned upon them.

They are from above, they cannot be predicted by no man yet they have been given power to control all things. Jesus reveals the origin of the new creature while having a private discussion with one of His secret disciples, Nicodemus. And I love how the Message Translation renders it:

> *Don't be so surprised when I tell you that you have to be 'born from above'—out of this world, so to speak. You know well enough how the wind blows this way and that. You hear it rustling through the trees, but you have no idea where it comes from or where it's headed next. That's the way it is with everyone 'born from above' by the wind of God, the Spirit of God.* **John 3:7-8 (Msg)**

Earthly Residents, Heavenly Citizens

In our world today, immigration has become one of the most challenging issues for governments all around the world. These governments have put strict policies and regulations in place that would prevent non-citizens of their countries from having access to the resources and benefits of the nation. For example, a Kenyan citizen residing legally in the Netherlands cannot have access to some benefits enjoyed by the Dutch citizen, because he is considered a resident and not a citizen. While residing in the Netherlands as a legal resident, he is entitled to the benefits of his home country, Kenya. Likewise, these new creatures are resident on the earth, but are heavenly citizens because they have been born from above.

Since they are heavenly citizens, they have been given full rights to all the resources of their country. There are benefits bequeathed to them by the reason of birth. It is an automatic access for any new creature, born into Christ and His kingdom. We are encouraged to come boldly before the throne to obtain mercy in times of need (Hebrews 14:16)

> *But we are citizens of heaven, where the Lord Jesus Christ lives. And we are eagerly waiting for him to return as our Savior.* **Philippians 3:20 (NLT)**

The new creatures can boldly walk in the light of the country they are from. They live in two dimensions at the same time, one spiritual and the other physical. Therefore, the Apostle Paul encourages the new creature to begin to walk in the consciousness of the country they are born into. They have to:

> *Set your mind on things above, not on earthly things.* **Colossians 3:20**

Paul, the apostle, explains the reason in another portion of the Scriptures, he said:

> *Therefore, you are no longer strangers and foreigners, but fellow citizens of the saints and members of God's household.* **Ephesians 2:19**

Unlike the children of Israel who were afraid to come near when God commanded Moses to bring the people to Mount Sinai. Apostle Paul was very careful to explain, that the new creatures have no cause to fear the environment where God resides because they are born in Zion. He is admonished to be bold about where he is from.

> *Now, you have come to Mount Zion, to the city of the living God, the heavenly Jerusalem, and to the countless thousands of angels in a joyful gathering. You have come to the assembly of God's firstborn children, whose names are written in heaven. You have come to God himself, who is the judge over all things. You have come to the spirits of the righteous ones in heaven who*

have not been made perfect. You have come to Jesus, the one who mediates the new covenant between God and people, and to sprinkled blood, which speaks of forgiveness instead of out for vengeance like the blood of Abel. **Hebrews 12:22-24 (NLT)**

This country is free from crime and decay. It is a place of abundance, peace, and blessings. The atmosphere is righteousness, and the air is love because their Savior hails from there. No one experiences death in this land because Life Himself is there with and for them. The new creatures enjoy the lavish splendor of the grace and glory of their God, despite their temporary location in time.

They Have a Language

These miraculous signs will accompany those who believe they will cast out demons in my name, and they will speak in new languages. **Mark 16:17 (NLT)**

Because they have a country where they are from, they have a language. This language is meant for direct communication with and to God, with no interception. The Holy Spirit, the Guide of the new creatures, brings and enables this language to them, and teaches them to improve on it as they grow in their faith. In the Book of Acts of the Apostles, this language was first released on a hundred and twenty new creatures gathered in one accord.

> And when the day of Pentecost was fully come, they were all with one accord in one place. And suddenly there came a sound from heaven as of a rushing mighty wind, and it filled all the house where they were sitting. And there appeared unto them cloven tongues like as of fire, and it sat upon each of them. And they were all filled with the Holy Ghost, and began to speak with other tongues, as the Spirit gave them utterance. **Acts 2:1-4.**

Because the new creatures are spirit beings, their communication has to be spiritual. Thus, the Lord blessed them with an amazing language that no mortal man can comprehend. There is nothing mortal or natural about this heavenly language called, "Tongues." They are edified and charged up personally as they speak in their heavenly language.

> He who speaks in a tongue edifies himself, but he who prophesies edifies himself. **1 Corinthians 14:4**

This language is higher than any known language of the mere men. It is the most "holy and pure" language of communicating with God. When a mere man prays, he does so from his mind, but the spirit of the new creatures prays when they pray. Paul argues this truth in his letters to the church at Corinth.

> *For if I pray in tongue, my spirit prays, but my understanding is unfruitful. What is the conclusion then? I will pray with the spirit, and I will also pray with the understanding. I will sing with the spirit, and I will also sing with the understanding.* **1 Corinthians 14:14-15**

The natural or mere man cannot understand, learn, speak or receive this language because it is enabled only by the Holy Spirit. And since they are not born again, and their bodies are considered not pure for the indwelling of the Holy Spirit, they are left to wonder what "tongues" are.

> *But the natural man receives not the things of the Spirit of God: for they are foolishness to him: neither can he know them, because they are spiritually discerned.* **1 Corinthians 2:14**

For an English man who travels to Saudi Arabia to do business without any translator, the Arabic language would sound unreasonable to him. The reaction of the first mere men, who heard this heavenly language when the Holy Spirit was poured out on the new creatures in the book of Acts, is the same today. The mere man makes a mockery of "tongues" because they consider it foolishness and it is spiritually discerned.

> *And there were dwelling at Jerusalem Jews, devout men, out of every nation under heaven. Now when this was noised abroad, the multitude came together, and were confounded, because every man heard them speak in his own language. And they were all amazed and marveled, saying one to another, Behold, are not all these which speak Galileans? And how hear we every man in our own tongue, wherein we were born? Parthians, Medes, and Elamites, and the dwellers in Mesopotamia, and in Judaea, and Cappadocia, in Pontus, and Asia, 10 Phrygia, and Pamphylia, in Egypt, and in the parts of Libya about Cyrene, and strangers of Rome, Jews and proselytes, Cretans and Arabians, we do hear them speak in our tongues the wonderful works of God. 1And they were amazed, and were in doubt, saying one to another, what does this mean? 13 Others mocking said, these men are full of new wine.*
> **Acts 2:5-13**

The closest description the mere men present at the day of Pentecost could give about this heavenly language is that of a speech of a drunkard. However, the new creatures supernaturally spoke in the natural languages of everyone present. Their mind couldn't grasp such a wonderful miracle. The Holy Spirit can enable a new creature to speak in a human language he has not learned before through tongues. The miracle of tongues cannot be described to a mere man.

They Cannot Be Sick

Because of the Divine life infused in them, the new creatures cannot get sick. There is not a place recorded in the Scriptures that Jesus (the Prototype) of the new creatures got sick. If the Prototype couldn't be sick, the rest made in His image couldn't be sick either.

Unfortunately, many of the new creatures still permit sickness to buffet their bodies. The lack of the right knowledge of the Word of God has seen to this mindset that has lingered since the days of the inception of the church. There are no Scriptural record of the Apostles being sick at any time. They understood these truths of the country from where they were born;

> *And no resident of Zion will say, "I am sick." The people who dwell there will be forgive their iniquity.* **- Isaiah 32: 4 (BSB)**

Once, I corrected a woman (a new creature), that she wasn't sick, as she boldly professed being sick. I said to her, that you feel the sickness in your natural body doesn't make you sick. You cannot declare, "I am blessed, and I am sick at the same time." There is no blessing in sickness. It is of the devil and it came about because of sin. The new creature has been delivered from the domain of darkness (Colossians 1:13), which includes all types and kinds of sicknesses. After our discussion, she understood that " the citizens of the beloved country

Zion, will never say, "I am sick," because they are never sick.

They Cannot Be Poor

Poverty is spiritual and very demonic. There is nothing good or fair about poverty. It is the breeding womb of all unimaginable wickedness. Poverty was also dealt with by our Lord and Savior Jesus Christ. In Zion (the country of origin of the new creatures), nothing is poor. How can the place the Almighty God dwells be associated with poverty? Therefore, His offspring were born into the abundance of wealth that the mind of the mortal man cannot comprehend. How can one created in the image of Christ be classified as poor? Any new creature that still embraces and operates in poverty is only ignorant of who he is and what has been made available to him. Poverty is not the lack of money as many have assumed, but it is a demonic spirit that has handicapped many and left them in a state of never having, scarcely having, barely having, never enough, and never productive. Jesus said about His purpose:

> *The thief's purpose is to steal and kill and destroy. My purpose is to give them a rich and satisfying life.* **John 10:10 (NLT)**

There is nothing rich and satisfying about poverty. So, the Lord Jesus Christ took a very drastic measure to fix this poverty situation, once and for all.

The life the new creature received after he was born again is rich, and there is no limit to this abundant life. Hence, the new creatures are rich, very rich. Sadly, so many still wallow in the pit of poverty with the claim that poverty is a good sign of humility.

> *For you are becoming progressively acquainted with and recognizing more strongly and clearly the grace of our Lord Jesus Christ (His kindness, His gracious generosity, His undeserved favor and spiritual blessing) [in] that though He was [so very] rich, yet for your sakes He became [so very] poor, in order that by His poverty you might become enriched (abundantly supplied).* **2 Corinthians 8:9 (AMP)**

There are supplies in abundance allocated to every new creature, living in this world now. And these supplies are not meant for when we get to heaven. They are given to us to be used in our daily lives. God wants His children comfortable, very comfortable. He doesn't take pleasure in poverty, that's the reason for the exchange Jesus did on the cross, the rich-for-the-poor and the -poor-for-the-rich. Why is the poor-made-rich still poor, after this great exchange?

Partakers of the Divine Nature

> *He hath given unto us exceeding great and precious promises: that by these you might be*

> *partakers of the Divine nature, having escaped the corruption that is in the world through lust.*
> **2 Peter 1:4**

Partakers of the Divine nature. This is a very bold statement to comprehend for many. And for others, this couldn't be possible or attainable. As bold and ridiculous these words may sound to many, they are only communicating the teaching of which the entire New Testament is full of; that mere men, by faith, can receive the life and nature of God and become brand new creatures. What does the teaching of regeneration or sons of God represent in Scriptures? In John 15 Christ publicly announced that He dwells in us and we in Him, as the branches, or what does "He that is joined with the Lord is one spirit (1 Corinthians 6:17) communicates to us?

Christ Jesus was sent by the Father into the world to save mere men, and to birth them by His Spirit as new creatures who are partakers of His divine nature. This means the new creatures share in the very blessings that the nature of God they have received bestows. It means that the new creature has been called into the arena or class of the Godkind. This class cannot be attained by any, except by being called and chosen by God Himself. And that's what He did, by His will He birthed the new creature in Christ, and by His own decisions they are partakers of His divine nature.

They Have Power

They have been given power and authority to influence everything in the natural and spiritual realms respectively. The new creature is an unpredictable being. He is like the wind, Jesus said; you can see the effect of the wind, but you can't see the wind. He is a strange species that cannot be figured out by the Adamic man. He is a "god" in every aspect because God made him so.

Only 'the gods of the earth' have authority and power. Since authority and power cannot be assumed but is given, the new creatures have been accorded all authority and power in the name of the first New Creature, the God-Man, Jesus Christ. In His name they are empowered to checkmate all things.

> *And I will give to you the keys of the kingdom of heaven: and what every you shall bind on earth shall be bound in heaven: and whatever you shall loose on earth shall be loosed on heaven.*
> **Matthew 16:19**

The new creatures have been given the keys of the kingdom of heaven. The keys to the kingdom of heaven are the access to the inheritance of Abraham through Christ and the eternal verities of the kingdom of God. The Greek word for 'keys' in the Bible verse is "Klao" and it means to shut, and this word can be used literally or figuratively. It is the word for example, to cause heaven to withhold rain or to obstruct someone or something.

Such great power is given to the new creature by Jesus Christ; the power to decide a thing and have it established. It means when the new creature decides concerning anything, Heaven has decided. Therefore, Heaven awaits them to make the call and it is as they have uttered, even when they declare judgment from their lips.

Job prophetically wrote about the authority of this new creature and the extent of the responsibilities bestowed upon them. The establishment of any matter or situation depends on their decisions, whatever they decide is and will become.

> *You will decide on a matter, and it will be established for you, and light will shine on your ways.* **Job 22:28 (ESV)**

Imagine a people with the keys to the kingdom of heaven and having the freedom to decide on any matter. The new creatures have been given such freedom; the greatest challenge of the new creatures is that they are yet to discover who God made them in Christ Jesus. They still wait on heaven to decide on a matter whilst heaven is waiting for them to give the green light. Many begin to function and act like mere men, thinking they are not having progress in their lives. As a new creature, your progress is not found in anybody's hands but yours. However you desire it, whichever height you decide to fly, it's attainable based on your own decision and faith.

God's Powerline

> *God has spoken once, twice have I heard this; that power belongs to God.* **Psalm 62:11**

We must understand that "power" belongs to God. It doesn't belong to any man, angel or any other being in any realm. Because it belongs to Him, He gives power to whomsoever He chooses to by His own qualifications. The obedience of Christ to the will of the Father, saw to it that God vested all His power in Jesus's name.

So therefore, after our Lord and Savior Jesus Christ rose from the grave, He made a profound and exciting statement to the eleven disciples and this applies to every one of His disciples. He said;

> *And Jesus came and spoke to them, saying, All power is given to me in heaven and in earth.* **Matthew 28:18**

That's amazing! All power that was, is, and will ever be, has been given to Jesus, thus, He is the Generating Source of all power, Power Personified! Because He is the Generating Source of all power, His disciples become the conduit of His power.

The life of the new creature is in Christ. He is now hidden in Christ, who is the Generating Source of all that the new creation is, including power. Christ is our power because we are hidden in Him.

> *If you then be risen with Christ, seek those things which are above, where Christ sits on the right hand of God. Set your affection on things above, not in things on the earth. For you are dead, and your life is hid with Christ in God. When Christ, who is our life, shall appear, then shall you also appear with Him in glory.* **Colossians 3:1-4**

The old you died when you gave your life to the Lord Jesus Christ, and now He is your life. Meaning that the life you possess in your spirit now doesn't belong to you, it is the life of Christ. Therefore, the new creatures are directly connected to the generating source of power which has become their life.

> *I have been crucified with Christ, and I longer live, but Christ lives in me. The life I live in the body, I live by faith in the Son of God, who loved me and gave Himself for me.* **Galatians 2:20**

For example in electricity, a power line is an electric wire, cable, or conduit suspended in the air by utility poles or transmission towers, or buried underground, used for supplying or carrying electricity either from a power source such as a generating station to a substation, or from a substation to a building such as a plant, commercial buildings or sometimes homes.

The new creature has become the power line of the power of God, and this power is tapped from Christ, The Generating Source. He has received this power for distribution, and changes lives and the world around him. lighting the dark world with the light of God he is and making a source that all darkness bows to the power of Christ in him.

The new creatures should never believe or accept that they are without power; they are loaded, the most dangerous beings walking on planet Earth. They should never believe the lies of the devil that they are weak and powerless. The new creature is joined, attached, submerged, and connected with Christ (1 Corinthians 6:17), Who is the Generating Source of our power. The new creature is the power line of God in the earth. He carries the power-current of God, to bring into subjection every power and all things, that are contrary and opposing to Christ, His Word and His Church.

Power and Authority

Although sometimes used interchangeably, power and authority have different meanings. They are not the same as believed by many. What is Power and what is Authority?

Power
It is the capacity or ability to direct or influence the behavior of others or the course of events. Power is always inherent, and because we are joined with Christ, His inherent power is available to us.

> But you shall receive power, after that the Holy Ghost is come on you: and you shall be witnesses to me both in Jerusalem, and in all Judaea, and in Samaria and unto the uttermost part of the earth. **Acts 1:8**

Authority
This is the right of attorney. Using one's power in his stead. It is also the moral or legal right or ability to control. The right to give orders, make decisions, and enforce obedience. Authority is always delegated. It is from one person to the other.

Jesus gave the twelve authority in His name to do ministry and to bring into subjection all the power of the enemy and nothing shall by any means hurt them.

> I have given you authority to tread on serpents and scorpions, and over all the power of the enemy, nothing will injure you. - **Luke 10:19 (NASB)**

It is therefore necessary to note that the new creature receives authority when he is born again, and power when he is filled with the Holy Spirit. The Holy Spirit is the Power of God and anyone who has Him, has received power.

Thus, the new creature can operate in authority and not in power. A person may have a firearm (a gun) to change the lives of people wrongly but doesn't have the authority to use such a firearm. But a police officer trained and equipped by the state or country he's working for has been given the right to have power and function in authority.

The Gospel, God's Power

After the new creature is born again and filled with the Holy Spirit, he now has the right to spread the gospel of Jesus Christ to his world. The gospel in and with the new creature is the very power of God. When this power (the Gospel) is transmitted to the unbelievers, they receive the signal or are opened for the reception and salvation is achieved.

> *For I am not ashamed of the gospel, because it is the power of God that brings salvation to everyone that believes, first to the Jews and then the Gentiles.* **Romans 1:16 (NIV)**

Furthermore,

> *The message of the cross is foolish to those who are headed for destruction! But we who are being saved know it is the very power of God.* **1 Corinthians 1:18 (NLT)**

It is this power that got us saved. And what we have received from the Lord, we pass on to the dying world, and changes are realized. As a power line, we are to transmit the power we've received from our Generating Source, (Jesus Christ), to the world.

Apostle Paul admonishing the brethren and releasing to them the revelation that he'd received from the Lord, wrote this:

> *For I received from the Lord what I also passed on to you* **1 Corinthians 11:23 (NIV)**

King-Priest

By virtue of the new life in Christ, the new creature has been made a king-priest. A king-priest is a two-fold-in-one office. In the Old Testament, they had the king and also the priest, separately. God designed it by lineage, in order to avoid confusion or someone usurping an office that wasn't meant for him. They had the kings from the lineage of Judah and the tribe of Levi produced the priest. But the new creature originates from Christ, that's his lineage, the generation of Christ Jesus. Thus, he is made a king and a priest unto God the Father—a twofold office (Revelation 1:6; 5:10). And because he is the righteousness of God in Christ Jesus, he is not just a king-priest but a righteous king-priest (Isaiah 32:1). The entire world, the devil and the hordes of hell and darkness are subdued before him in the name of Jesus.

The new creature is reigning in righteousness and in Christ, God have made him ruler over the works of His hands.

> *And from Jesus Christ, who is the faithful witness, and the first begotten of the dead, and the prince of the kings of the earth. Unto him that loved us, and washed us from our sins in his own blood. And hath made us kings and priests unto God and his Father; to him be glory and dominion forever and ever, Amen.* **Revelation 1:5-6**

They Know the Works of God

The new creature is not in the same class as the Adamic or mere men. Therefore, the Adamic man is the one whom God put eternity in his heart yet limited to know the works of God. Ecclesiastes 3:11b explains that "... so that no man can find out the work that God does from the beginning to the end." Only the mere man can't find out the work God does from the beginning. The new creature can.

Since the class of the new creature is higher. As mentioned earlier, Eternity was not put in his heart, he was born in and with it. He can find out the works of God because of the Holy Spirit of God who now dwells in him. Unlike the Adamic man there is no limitation whether spiritual or natural, he can always know the mind of God and His plans and purposes.

> *But as it is written, eye has not seen, nor ear heard, neither have entered into the heart of man, the things which God has prepared for them that love Him. But God has revealed them to us by His Spirit: for the Spirit searches all things, yes, the deep things of God. For what man knows the things of a man, save the spirit of man which is in him? Even so, the things of God knows no man, but the Spirit of God. Now, we have received, not the spirit of the world, but the Spirit which of God; that we might know the things which are freely given to us of God. Which things also we speak, not in the words which man's wisdom teaches, but which the Holy Ghost teaches, comparing spiritual things Vwith spiritual. But the natural man receives not the things of the Spirit of God: for they are foolishness to him: neither can he know them because they are spiritually discerned. But he that is spiritual judges all things, yet he himself is judged of no man. For who has known the mind of the Lord, that he may instruct Him? But we have the mind of Christ.* **1 Corinthians 2:9-16**

It doesn't matter how highly and profoundly educated the mere man is, he cannot know the works of God because they are spiritually discerned, and since he is spiritually dead unto God and His works, he considers God's work as foolishness. The Adamic man cannot see or hear and does not have the ability and capacity to receive what God has prepared for those [the new creatures] who love Him. But to the new creature they are revealed by His Spirit, because the Holy Spirit is God Himself indwelling the New Creature, He searches the deep things of God and reveals His works to the new creature. The new creature is considered spiritual and has the right to judge all things and yet judge no man. He knows all that is freely given to him by God, because he is one with the Lord now; his spirit is joined with the Lord's.

The Prototype of the New Creatures

Christ Jesus is the prototype of how the new creatures should be and look like. Because Christ Jesus is the lamb that was slain before the foundation of the world (Revelation 13:8). This means God defined and saw the prototype before Adam was created. Therefore, God's utmost intention was not the mere man but the new creature who is the same as the prototype.

In the car manufacturing industry and also in other manufacturing sectors, before a particular product goes into production and ends up with the consumer, the manufacturer will develop a prototype that will become the model for the rest of the production of this particular product. Firstly, the prototype must go through all kinds of procedures and tests to be certified as worthy for production. After the manufacturer is satisfied with the prototype, large-scale production begins using the prototype as the gauge to measure and determine the quality of the rest of the products. Whatever is found in the prototype is duplicated in the rest. Whatever is found in the rest of the production and is not part of the prototype is considered an error in production. That product will ultimately not make it to the marketplace and will be discarded.

Most manufacturers invest a lot of money, time, and effort to get the prototype right. All other production of this particular product depends on the first example. And the prototype is always a top secret for the manufacturers. The success of the products depends on how little their competitors and others know about the prototype.

> *Beloved, now are we the sons of God, and it doth not yet appear what we shall be: but we know that, when he shall appear, we shall be like him; for we shall see him as he is.* **1 John 3:2**

Christ is the model by which God (the Manufacturer) births (produces) the new creatures by His Spirit. Everything in Christ is exactly how the new creature is created to be, although many are yet to come to this understanding. Because "if the first fruit be holy, the lump is also holy: and if the root be holy, so are the branches (Romans 11:16). So, the principle is parallel whether physical or spiritual. The new creature must be the exact copy or representation of the original prototype, that is Christ.

God the Father waited patiently for Christ to go through all He went through to become the first begotten from the dead.

The First-Born from the Dead

John reveals at the beginning of the Book of Revelation, the concept of Christ being the firstborn (in other words prototype). Addressing the churches who are birthed to be exactly like the firstborn.

> *Grace to you and the peace from him who is and who was and who is to come, and from the seven spirits who are before his throne, and from Jesus Christ the faithful witness,* **the firstborn of the dead**, *and the ruler of the kings of the earth.* **Revelation 1:4**

The Greek word for "firstborn" that John uses is *prototokos*, a word that literally explains birth order—the first child born. The place of the firstborn is of great importance in the Old Testament, where the firstborn inherits his father's place as the head of the family, receiving the father's blessing, and approval to lead the rest of the family and also receives the double portion of his inheritance (Deuteronomy 21:17). Metaphorically, the concept of the firstborn also refers to the special status of the firstborn as the preeminent son and heir (the prototype of the new creatures).

In the New Testament Jesus fulfills the role of God's faithful firstborn Son, in His perfect life, sacrificial death, and glorious resurrection. In God's plan, everything the firstborn is, the rest should be also. There are many other references in the New Testament where Jesus is referred to as *prototokos*, the firstborn.

> *For those whom he foreknew he also predestined to be conformed to the image of his Son, in order that he might be the firstborn among many brothers.* **Romans 8:29**

The predestination of those God foreknew was to be conformed, to be like the image of the firstborn Son, Christ Jesus. Why? Because He is the image of the invincible God, the firstborn of all creation (Colossians 1:15). Thus, the new creature has no business living like they are from the Adamic lineage, the consciousness of whom God has made them to be must become their reality.

> *He is the head of the body, the church. He is the beginning, the firstborn from the dead, that in all things he might be preeminent.* **Colossians 1:18**

Because He is the "firstborn from the dead," Christ Jesus is both first in time and in preeminence. As the first to be raised from spiritual death, He became the founder and prototype of the new era. This privilege is granted to everyone who is born again—to be spiritually alive to God, never again to taste death. The new creature holds the guarantee that, being in Christ and created like Him, we will reign with Him as the firstborn of God and heirs of all things in heaven and on earth.

> *But now Christ is risen from the dead, and has become the first fruits of those who have fallen asleep. For since by man came death, by Man also came the resurrection of the dead. For as in Adam all died, even so in Christ all shall be made alive. But each of his own order: Christ the first fruits, afterward those who are Christ's at His coming.* **1 Corinthians 15:20-23**

Knowing this reality, no new creature in Christ should live their lives below the standard of the Manufacturer (God, the Father). The intention of the Manufacturer for the production of the product must be fulfilled. The new creatures are God's product. We have been made with the same material (the Word) as the Prototype (Christ), thus there is no reason for every one of us to live below the standard He has created us to be in Christ Jesus. Therefore, whatever is not found in Christ is an error in your life. Sicknesses, poverty, shame, and all evil vices couldn't attach themselves to our Christ because of the Material He is and was made from (The Word of God). We are made from the same material as Him, His Word, therefore we cannot afford to tolerate whatever the devil and the world throws our path. The Prototype triumphed and gave us the victory, we must now maintain that victory in our lives, daily.

Luminaries

> *Ye are the light of the world. A city set on a hill that cannot be hid.* - **Matthew 5:14**

This very profound statement was made about the new creatures by our Lord Jesus Christ Himself. Contrary to any other definition the world may attach to the new creatures, Jesus explained to His disciples that they are the very reason the world is not in total darkness.

Without the new creatures the world will be in spiritual darkness, without the disciples of Jesus in the world the devil will have his way without restriction. The new creatures are the ones that put a check on the onslaught of the evil ones. By our continuous presence in the world, our prayers and intercessions, the plans of the devil and his hordes of demons are frustrated.

The new creatures must understand who they are and their place in the world. They are the ones God has put in charge to lead. They must take charge of the position that God has bestowed upon them and begin to shine the light they are in the world.

Luminaries Defined

Luminaries are celestial bodies, such as the Sun or Moon, a body, an object that gives light, a leading light. It also means a person who leads and others follows because of their prominence. A personality that is well-known or enlightening to mankind.

Every New creature, a Luminary

Every new creature is a luminary because God the Father made him so. When an individual, once in darkness, surrenders their heart to the Lord Jesus Christ, they are transformed into light—a luminary that reflects the light and glory of the Father in the world.

As new creatures we are the "leading lights," we have been called to lead while others follow. The light within us is neither of nor for ourselves; it is of God and for the world. Therefore, our calling is not to hide this light, but to shine in such a way that others may witness our good works and glorify the Father.

A hidden light is a useless light and is not worthy to be called a light. A leading light is supposed to be ahead of others showing the path that they must follow. It shines ahead and others can see, follow, and emulate. A luminary is that light that reflects what others should do and what they could become. The Lord Jesus said in the concluding part of His message in

Matthew 5:15-16

> *Neither do men light a lamp, and put it under a bushel, but on the lamp stand; and it gives light to all that are in the house. Let your light so shine before men, that they may see your good works and glorify your Father which is in heaven."*

The new creatures are called to be on the lamp stand, and they give their light to "all men" that are in the house (world). We must not choose who we should shine our lights before because our light is meant to be shone before all men in the world, no exemptions.

If men would not light a candle and put it under the bushel, but rather on the lamp stand, why would God make you light and hide you from men? The Father desires that our light "so shine" that because of the light you are, men would see your good works and glorify your Father who is in heaven. It is because of your light that men (mere men) would see, thus without shining so bright the purpose of the light is defeated.

> *The path of the righteous is as a shining light, that shines brighter and brighter unto the perfect day.* **Proverbs 4:18**

As luminaries, we provide solutions to the world's problems. The world's problem is spiritual and The Solution is also spiritual, Jesus is that Solution. Hence, the question is not whether we are light, but whether we shine. While we have been made lights, the responsibility to shine is something we must actively enforce and fulfill. And as we do, the brightness intensifies day by day unto the perfect day (the day we are with Jesus forever). And on and from that day, the bodies of the new creatures will glow and bring forth light. But before that becomes the reality we are called as luminaries to arise and shine our light.

> *Arise, shine; for thy light is come, and the glory of the Lord is risen upon thee.* **Isaiah 60:1**

To arise and shine implies taking action—to manifest who you already are. There is no shining without rising. Do you desire to radiate as the luminary you are? Take action and shine.

It is the earnest desire of the Father to see all of His children shine. He takes pleasure in our shining. He has made all things available for His new creatures to be the leading lights, radiating and beaming so brightly that no darkness can ever withstand. It is no longer an issue of shining but about the intensity (Voltage) of your shinning. Because the Father has called us into the category of the "so shine" luminaries we are.

Chapter Five

Biblical Truths About The New Creatures

In the Scriptures, profound differences between the new creatures and mere men are abundantly evident. They look the same on the outside, but there is a clear and profound spiritual difference between them. The new creature is a new creation, superior to Satan, his cohorts, and the world. He is one who has been brought into the God class, by the reason of the divine nature that he is a partaker of. He is the light in the world that expels all darkness, he is powerful, one like no other in all the creation of God. Because he was created in Christ Jesus, he bears the image of Christ, which is the image of God.

The mere mortal is a living soul, subject to the antics and chains of the devil. He belongs to the kingdom of darkness and has no place or inheritance in God. God in His infinite mercy has made a Way for all mere men to become new creatures. Left with the right to choose, they are already condemned if they reject so wonderful Gift of God to all mankind.

Truths

1. The new creature is born of God. He is the offspring of God Himself. The Mere man hails from Adam and is cut off from God

   Children born not of blood, nor of the desire or will of man, but born of God. **John 1:13**

   Everyone who believes that Jesus is Christ is born of God, and everyone who loves the Father also loves the one born of Him. **1 John 5:1**

2. The New Creature has overcome the world and he that is in the world by default. Just because he is God's offspring, he is a victor over the worldly system. While the Mere man is subject to the world and its system, he is a slave to the devil and his kingdom.

   For whoever is born of God overcomes the world: and this is the victory that overcomes the world, even our faith. **1 John 5:4**

   You, little children, are from God and have overcome them, because greater is He who is in you than he who is in the world. **1 John 4:4**

3. The new creature is from the Lord Jesus Christ who is the Quickening Spirit. Therefore, he is also a quickening spirit. The mere man is a living soul like Adam.

   And so, it is written, the first man Adam became a living soul; the last Adam was made a quickening Spirit. However, that was not the first which is spiritual, but that which is natural; and afterward that which is spiritual. The first man is of the earth, earthy: the second man is the Lord from Heaven. As is the earthy, such are they also that are earthy: and as is the heavenly, such are they also that are heavenly. And as we have borne the image of the earthy, we shall also bear the image of the heavenly. **1 Corinthians 15:45-49**

   For just as the Father raises the dead and gives them life, so also the Son gives life to whom He wishes. **John 5:21**

4. The new creature is a partaker of the Divine nature of God. He has been brought into the class of the Godkind. Although he could not attain this level by himself, God "brought" him into this class because of the Sacrifice of His Son Jesus Christ. The mere man is a mortal, one who is stripped of his dominion-ship.

   Whereby are given to us exceeding great and precious promises: that by these you might be partakers of the divine nature, having escaped the corruption that is in the world through lust. **2 Peter 1:4**

Beloved, we are now children of God, and what we will be has not yet been revealed, we know that when Christ appears, we will be like Him, for we will see him as He is. **1 John 3:2**

5. The new creatures are like Christ in this world. Thus, it is accurate to call them the Jesuses of their time. The mere men are Adams.

   I have given them the glory You gave Me, so that they may be one as We are One. **John 17:22**

   Herein is our love made perfect, that we may have boldness in the day of judgment: because as He is, so are we in this world. **1 John 4:17**

6. The new Creatures are children of God. God is the Father (Creator) of all spirits, but it is those who are born again that He calls His children. The Mere men are not His children until they get born again.

   Behold what manner of love the Father has given to us, that we should be called children of God. And that is what we are! The reason the world doesn't know us is that it did not know Him **1 John 3:1**

But to all who did receive Him, to those who believed on His name, He gave the right to become children of God. **John 1:12**

For as many as are led by the Spirit of God, they are the sons of God. For you have not received the spirit of bondage again to fear; but you have received the Spirit of adoption, whereby we cry Abba, Father. The Spirit Himself bears witness with our spirit, that we are the children of God. **Romans 8:14-16**

So, it is not the children of the flesh who are God's children, but it is the children of the promise who are regarded as offspring. **Romans 9:8**

And, I will be a Father to you, and you will be My sons and daughters, says the Lord Almighty. **1 Corinthians 6:18**

7. The new creature is joint heirs with Christ. He has a hundred percent right to all that belong to God Like Jesus Christ. Since the mere man is not a child of God, he cannot be heir to the promises of God in Christ Jesus.

   And if children, then heirs; heirs of God, and joint-heirs with Christ; if so be that we suffer with Him, that we may be also glorified together. **Romans 8:17**

Therefore, you are no longer a slave, but a son; and if a son, then an heir through God. **Galatians 4:7**

8. The new creatures are led by the Spirit of God. The mere man is led by his instincts and prone to being led by demonic forces.

   As many as are led by the Spirit of God, they are the sons of God. **Romans 8:14**

   But if you are led by the Spirit, you are not under the Law. **Galatians 5:18**

   And you He made alive, who were dead in trespasses and sins, in which you once walked according to the course of this world, according to the power of the air, the spirit who now works in the sons of disobedience. **Ephesians 2:1-2**

9. There is no condemnation or damnation for the new creature, because he has made peace with God through Jesus Christ. The mere man is already, condemned and judged unless he turns around accepts Jesus Christ as his Lord and Savior.

   For God did not send His Son into the world to condemn the world, but that the world through Him might be saved. He who believes in Him is not condemned; but he who does not believe is condemned already, because he has not believed in the name of the only begotten Son of God. And this is the condemnation, that the light has come into the world, and men loved darkness rather than light, because their deeds were evil. **John 3:17-19**

There is therefore now no condemnation to them who are in Christ Jesus. **Romans 8:1**

10. The new creature is spiritually alive to God and His works, while the mere man is spiritually dead and separated to God.

    And you He made alive, who were dead in trespasses and sins, in which you once walked according to the course of this world, according to the power of the air, the spirit who now works in the sons of disobedience. **Ephesians 2:1-2**

    For if by the one man's offense death reigned through the one, much more those who receive abundance of grace and the gift of righteousness will reign in life through the One, Jesus Christ. Therefore, as through one man's offense judgment came to all men, resulting in condemnation, even so through one Man's righteous act the free gift came to all men, resulting in justification of life. For as by one man's disobedience, many were made sinners, so also by one Man's obedience many will be made righteous. Moreover, the law entered that offense might abound. But where sin abounded, grace abounded much more, so that as sin reigned in death, even so grace might reign through righteousness to eternal life through Jesus Christ our Lord. **Romans 5:17-21**

11. The new creature has peace with God. He is in the blessed assurance of God's multiplied grace and ever abounding peace. The mere man is an enemy of God.

    Therefore, being justified by faith, we have peace with God through our Lord Jesus Christ. **Romans 5:1**

    And through Him to reconcile to Himself all things, whether things on earth or things in heaven, by making peace through the blood of His cross. **Colossians 1:20**

    You adulterers and adulteresses, know you not that the friendship of the world is enmity with God? Whoever therefore will be a friend of the world is the enemy of God **James 4:4**

12. The prayer of the new creature is avails much and it's a sweet-smelling odor before God. Unless it is the prayer of salvation, the prayer of the mere man is an abomination before God.

The sacrifice of the wicked is an abomination to the Lord: but the prayer of the upright is his delight. **Proverbs 15:8**

Confess your trespasses to one another, and pray for one another, that you may be healed. The effective, fervent prayer of a righteous man avails much. **James 5:16**

Let my prayer be set forth before you as incense; and the lifting up my hands as the evening sacrifice. **Psalm 141:2**

When He had taken the scroll, the four living creatures and the twenty-four elders fell down before the Lamb. Each had a harp, and they were holding golden bowls full of incense, which are the prayers of the saints. **Revelation 5:8**

Then another angel, who had a golden censer, came and stood at the altar. He was given much incense to offer, along with the prayers of all the saints, on the golden altar before the throne. And the smoke of the incense, together with the prayers of the saints, rose up before God from the hand of the angel. **Revelation 8:3-4**

13. The new creature is the temple of the Holy Spirit. He is God's abode and heaven's address on earth. The mere man is a potential habitation of demons and evil. Demons have the liberty to possess them

because they are not in the kingdom jurisdiction of God.

Do you not know that you yourselves are God's temple and that God's Spirit dwells in you? **1 Corinthians 3:16**

What? Know you not that your body is the temple of the Holy Ghost which is in you, which you have of God, and you are not your own? **1 Corinthians 6:19**

You, however, are controlled not by the flesh, but by the Spirit, if the Spirit of God lives in you. And if anyone does not have the Spirit of Christ, he does not belong to Christ. **Romans 8:9**

14. Righteousness is now the nature of the new creature. Through Christ Jesus he was made righteous. The mere man is a sinner.

    It is because of Him that you are in Christ Jesus, who has become for us wisdom from God: our righteousness, holiness, and redemption. **1 Corinthians 1:30**

    For He was made sin for us, who knew no sin; that we might be made the righteousness of God in Him. **1 Corinthians 5:21**

And be found in him, not having my own righteousness, which is of the law, but that which is through the faith of Christ, the righteousness which is of God by faith. **Philippians 3:9**

15. The new creature is powerful, full of power, and been given authority over all things. The mere man has no authority given to him. He could operate with the powers of darkness, but all the powers of darkness are subject to the authority given to the new creature in the name of Jesus.

    Truly I say to you, whatever you shall bind on earth shall be bound in heaven: and whatever you shall loose on earth shall be loosed in heaven. **Matthew 18:18**

    Behold, I give you power to tread on serpents and scorpions, and over all the power of the enemy: and nothing shall by any means hurt you. **Luke 10:19**

    They will pick up snakes with their hands, and if they drink any deadly poison, it will not harm them; they will lay their hands on the sick, and they will be made well. **Mark 16:18**

    You will tread on the lion and cobra; you will trample the young lion and serpent. **Psalm 91:13**

16. Because he is now a friend of God, the secret of the Lord is with the new creature. The mere man doesn't know God or His ways. God has no friendship with him until he gets born again.

    The secret of the Lord is with them who fear Him; He will show them His covenant. **Psalm 25:14**

    He shall glorify Me: for He shall receive of mine, and shall show it to you. All things that the Father has are Mine: Therefore said I, that He shall take of Mine and shall show it to you. **John 16:14-15**

17. The creature has the authority and legal right to judge all things. The mere man is already judged by all things in the system of the world, that he is in, which is run by the devil.

    Evil men do not understand justice, but those who seek the Lord comprehend fully. **Proverbs 28:5**

    But he that is spiritual judges all things, yet he himself is judged of no man. **1 Corinthians 2:15**

    You, however, have an anointing from the Holy One, and all of you know the truth. **1 John 2:20**

18. Although he resides temporally on earth, the new creature is a citizen of heaven. The mere man is the citizen of the earthly nations and, unfortunately,

will spend his eternity, separated from God in the lake of fire, with the devil and his angels.

As was the earthly man, so also are those who are of the earth; and as is the heavenly man, so also are those who are of heaven. **1 Corinthians 15:48**

For our citizenship is in heaven; from which also we look for the Savior, the Lord Jesus Christ. **Philippians 3:20**

Therefore, you are no longer strangers and foreigners, but fellow citizens of the saints and members of God's household. **Ephesians 2:19**

Instead, you have come to Mount Zion, to the city of the living God, the heavenly Jerusalem. You have come to myriads of angels. **Hebrews 12:22**

19. The new creature is an ambassador of God's kingdom on earth. The mere man is an ambassador of the worldly systems. He is a worker of evil before God.

Now then we are ambassadors for Christ, as though God did beseech you by us: we pray you in Christ's stead, be you reconciled to God. **1 Corinthians 5:20**

As God's fellow workers, we urge you not to receive God's grace in vain. **2 Corinthians 6:1**

Who also has made us able ministers of the new covenant; not of the letter, but of the Spirit: for the letter kills, but the Spirit gives life. **2 Corinthians 3:6**

For which I am an ambassador in chains. Pray that I may proclaim if fearlessly, as I should. **Ephesians 6:20**

20. Christ is made unto him wisdom, so the new creature is full of divine wisdom. The mere man has intellectual wisdom which is from the systems of the world.

    For I will give you a mouth and wisdom, which all of your adversaries shall not be able to gainsay nor resist. **Luke 21:15**

    But of Him are you in Christ Jesus, who of God is made unto us wisdom, and righteousness, and sanctification, and redemption. **1 Corinthians 1:30**

    Let the word of Christ richly dwell within you, with all wisdom teaching and admonishing one another in psalms and hymns and spiritual songs, singing with grace in your hearts to the Lord. **Colossians 3:16**

21. The new creature is one Spirit with the Lord because he is now joined with Him. He is one with Adam. He lives and operates in the soulish realms. He is now one Spirit with the Lord. Because the new creature is joined with the Lord Jesus Christ by reason of regeneration. He is now one with the Lord. As long as he remains unrepentant the mere man is very Adamic, and this reflects in the entirety of his being.

   But he that is joined to the Lord is one spirit with Him. **1 Corinthians 6:17**

   That all of them may be one, as You, Father, are in Me, and I in You. May they also be one in Us, so that the world may believe that you have sent Me. **John 17:21**

   I have been crucified with Christ, and I no longer live, but Christ lives in me. The life I live in the body, I live by the faith in the Son of God, who loved me and gave Himself for me. **Galatians 2:20**

22. The new creature has the mind of Christ. He judges, discerns, and approves all things rightly because he received the mind of Christ when he was born again. Through the Word of God, this mind is developed to maturity. Therefore, he is also called not to be conformed to this world but to be transformed by the renewing of his mind, this can only be achieved

by the Word of God (Romans 12:2). But the mere man cannot receive the mind of Christ- his mind is limited to the Adamic mind.

Let this mind be in you which was also in Christ Jesus. **Philippians 2:5**

For who has known the mind of the Lord, that he may instruct him? But we have the mind of Christ **1 Corinthians 2:16**

23. The new creature belongs to Christ Jesus and His kingdom. The Spirit of Christ—the Holy Spirit is the Spirit of Christ and He dwells in the new creature as a proof of Christ's ownership. The mere man doesn't belong to Christ, he belongs to the world and its realm.

You, however, are controlled not by the flesh, but by the Spirit, if the Spirit of God lives in you. And if anyone does not have the Spirit of Christ, he does not belong to Christ. **Romans 8:9**

Do you not know that your body is a temple of the Holy Spirit who lives in you, whom you have received from God? You are not your own. **2 Corinthians 6:16**

And what agreement hath the temple of God with idols? For ye are the temple of the living God; as God hath said, I will dwell in them, and walk in them; and I will be their God, and they shall be my people. **1 Corinthians 6:16**

24. The new creature is not controlled by his flesh or the dictates of his environment. He is led by the Spirit of God. The mere man is always led and controlled by his intellect and desires.

    You, however, are controlled not by the flesh, but by the Spirit, if the Spirit of God lives in you. And if anyone does not have the Spirit of Christ, he does not belong to Christ. **Romans 8:9**

    For as many as are led the by Spirit of God, they are the sons of God. For you have not received the spirit of bondage again to fear; but you have received the Spirit of adoption, whereby we cry, Abba, Father. **Romans 8:14-15**

25. The new creature is made holy after being born again and, therefore is qualified to house the Holy Spirit. His spirit now has the capacity and ability to commune with the Spirit of God. The mere man is dead spiritually to God and cannot receive the Holy Spirit.

    Even the Spirit of truth; whom the world cannot receive, because it sees Him not, neither knows Him: but you know Him; for He dwells with you and shall be in you. **John 14:17**

We are from God. Whoever knows God listens to us; whoever is not from God does not listen to us. That is how we know the Spirit of truth and the spirit of deception. **1 John 4:6**

26. The new creature is led by the Spirit of Truth, while the mere man is led by the spirit of deception.

    We are from God. Whoever knows God listens to us; whoever is not from God does not listen to us. That is how we know the Spirit of truth and the spirit of deception. **1 John 4:6**

    However, when the Spirit of truth comes, he will guide you into all truth. For He will not speak on His own, but He will speak what He hears, and He will declare to you what is to come. **John 16:13**

27. The new creatures are seated in Christ, far above every power. Because we are His Body, the Church and He is the Head of the body, we are one with Him. And He is seated far above all powers. We have received the legal right to exercise authority over powers and thrones that be. the mere man is defenseless to the stratagems and plots of the devil. He is altogether powerless.

    Far above all principalities and power and might and dominion, and every name that is named, not only in the age but also in that which is to come. And He put all things under His feet, and gave Him to be the head over all things to the church, which is His body, the fullness of Him who fills all in all. **Ephesians 1:21-23**

And you have been made complete in Christ, who is the Head over every ruler and authority. **Colossians 2:10**

His purpose was that now, through the church, the manifold wisdom of God should be made known to the rulers and authorities in the heavenly realms. **Ephesians 3:10**

28. The new creature has the right to use the name of Jesus as a weapon to command and affect change, subdue demonic rulers and power, command elements and their courses and they all will obey. The name of Jesus does not respond to the mere man- he is not called or owned by the One behind the name.

    The name of the Lord is a strong tower: the righteous runs into it and is safe. **Proverbs 18:10**

    Wherefore God also hath highly exalted him and given him a name which above every name: That at the name of Jesus every knee should bow, of things in heaven, and things in earth, and things under the earth; And that every tongue should confess that Jesus Christ is Lord, to the glory of God the Father. **Philippians 2:9-11**

> *So that the name of our Lord Jesus will be glorified in you, and you in Him, according to the grace of our God and of the Lord Jesus Christ.* **2 Thessalonians 1:12**

29. The new man triumphs always in all things, he is more than a conqueror, because he is born of God. The mere man is always under the whip of the devil and his worldly systems.

> *But thanks be unto God, which gives us the victory through our Lord Jesus Christ.* **1 Corinthians 15:57**

> *Now thanks be unto God, who always causes us to triumph in Christ, and makes manifest the fragrance of his knowledge by us in every place.* **2 Corinthians 2:14**

> *For whoever is born of God overcomes the world: and this is the victory that overcomes the world, even our faith.* **1John 5:4**

> *Yet, in all these things we are more than conquerors through him that loved us.* **Romans 8:37**

30. Because all things work together for his good, the new creature cannot be disadvantaged. It doesn't matter how terrible and unfair it may appear. It will always turn around for his good. The mere man is

at the mercy of chance, he can be disadvantaged **Psalm 37:1-36**

And we know that all things work together for good to them that love God, to them who are the called according to his purpose. **Romans 8:28**

Having made known to us the mystery of His will, according to His good pleasure which He purposed in Himself, that in the dispensation of times, He might gather in one all things in Christ, both which are in heaven and which are on earth—in Him. In Him also we have obtained an inheritance, being predestined according to the purpose of Him who works all things according to the counsel of His will, that we who first trusted in Christ should be to the praise of His glory. **Ephesians 1:9-12**

31. The new creature has been delivered and rescued, from the kingdom of darkness. He doesn't need deliverance. He has already been delivered when he got born again. He is now in the Kingdom of God. The mere man is still in the domain of darkness, and he is always at their mercy.

    Who has delivered us from the power of darkness and has translated us into the kingdom of His dear Son. **Colossians 1:13**

For as much then as the children are partakers of flesh and blood, He also Himself likewise took part of the same; that through His death He might destroy him that had the power of death, that is, the devil. **Hebrews 2:14**

32. The new creatures are the light of the world. In the eyes of the Almighty God, the world is darkness, therefore, His children are the only light on the earth that He sees and acknowledges. Everything the mere man is and represents is darkness before the Lord God Almighty. He must embrace Jesus, the Light of the world.

The path of the righteous is like the first gleam of dawn, shining brighter and brighter until midday. **Proverbs 4:18**

You are the light of the world. A city that is set on a hill cannot be hid. **Matthew 5:14**

While you have the Light, believe in the Light, so that you may become the sons of light. After Jesus had spoken these things, he went away and was hidden from them. **John 12:36**

So that you may be blameless and pure, children of God without fault in a crooked and perverse generation, in which you shine as lights in the world. **Philippians 2:12**

33. The new creatures are kings and priests to God. They have been chosen by the reason of the Blood of Christ Jesus. Everything they offer unto God is considered hallowed. The offering of the mere man is an abomination unto the Lord.

They will be Mine, says the Lord of Host, on the day when I prepare My treasured possession. And I will spare them as a man spares his own son who serves him. **Malachi 3:17**

But you are a chosen generation, a royal priesthood, an holy nation, a peculiar people; that you should show forth the praises of him who has called you out of darkness into his marvelous light. **1 Peter 2:9**

He gave Himself for us to redeem us from all lawlessness and to purify for Himself a people for His own possession, zealous for good works. **Titus 2:14**

And hath made us kings and priests unto God and his Father; to him be glory and dominion forever and ever. Amen **Revelation 1:6**

34. The new creature has an inheritance and has been given the right of claim to this inheritance in God by Jesus Christ. Because he is Abraham's seed, the blessings of Abraham are attributed to his account. The mere man is a total stranger to the

commonwealth of the kingdom of God, he has no part in God's inheritance.

Giving thanks to the Father, which has made us meet to be partakers of the inheritance of the saints in light. **Colossians 1:12**

To open their eyes, so that they may turn from darkness to light and from the power of Satan to God, that they may receive forgiveness of sins and an inheritance among those sanctified by faith in Me. **Acts 26:18**

I ask that the eyes of your heart may be enlightened, so that you may know the hope of His calling, the riches of His glorious inheritance in the saints. **Ephesians 1:18**

35. The new creature is saved and safe for eternity. The mere man is already damned. It is never the will and pleasure of God to have anyone man condemned, but by refusing the Only WAY out, the mere man already incurred condemnation on himself.

Have I any pleasure at all that the wicked should die? Says the Lord God: and not that he should turn from his ways, and live? **Ezekiel 18:23**

He that believes and is baptized shall be saved, but he that believes not shall be condemned. **Mark 16:16**

Whoever believes in Him is not condemned, but whoever does not believe has already been condemned, because he has not believed in the name of God's one and only Son. **John 3:18**

Whoever believes in the Son has eternal life. Whoever rejects the Son will not see life. Instead, the wrath of God remains on him **John 3:36**

36. The new creature is reigning in this life and will also reign in the life to come. The mere man is separated from God and cannot reign in this life or in that which is to come.

    For if by one's offense death reigned by one; much more they which receive abundance of grace and of the gift of righteousness shall reign in life by one, Jesus Christ. **Romans 5:17**

    There will be no more night in the city, and they will have no need for the light of a lamp or the sun. for the Lord God will shine on them and they will reign forever and ever. **Revelation 22:5**

37. The new creature has the capacity to live, walk, express, show, and communicate the Love of God. The mere man can't give what he doesn't have. He can only experience the love of God that He has already shown to the world through His Son Jesus Christ. **John 13:34:**

A new commandment I give to you, that you love one another, even as I have loved you, that you also love one another. **John 13:34**

And walk in love, just as Christ also loved you and gave Himself up for us, an offering and a sacrifice to God as a fragrant aroma **Ephesians 5:2**

Beyond all these things put on love, which is the perfect bond of unity. **Colossians 3:14**

38. The new creature has the privilege to be a leader over the flock of God in the Body of Christ. The mere man cannot be a leader in the house of God unless he becomes born again.

    Then I will give you shepherds after My own heart, who will feed you with knowledge and understanding. **Jeremiah 3:15**

    And He gave some apostles; and some, prophets; and some, evangelists; and some, pastors and teachers; for the perfecting of the saints, for the work of the ministry, for the edifying of the body of Christ: till we all come in the unity of faith, and the knowledge of the Son of God, to a perfect man, to the measure of the stature of the fullness of Christ. **Ephesians 4:11-13**

    And in the church God has appointed first of all apostles, second prophets, third teachers, then workers of miracles, and those with gifts of healing, helping, administration, and various tongues. **1 Corinthians 12:28**

39. The new creature is a minister, an instrument of change, God's mouthpiece to the world. The mere man cannot be God's authorized mouthpiece.

   Let no man so account of us, as of the ministers of Christ, and stewards of the mysteries of God. Moreover, it is required in stewards that a man be found faithful. **1 Corinthians 4:1-2**

   If any man speak, let him speak as the oracles of God; if any man minister, let him do it as of the ability which God gives: that God in all things may be glorified through Jesus Christ, to whom be praised in dominion forever and ever. Amen **1 Peter 4:11**

40. The new creature is in right standing with God. Righteousness is right standing with God. It doesn't mean "perfection" The new creature is righteous because God gave him the gift of righteousness and declared him to be righteous in Him through Christ. The mere man doesn't have a right standing with God because he is still considered a sinner before God.

   Yet God, in His grace, freely makes us right in His sight. He did this through Christ Jesus when He freed us from the penalty for our sins. **Romans 3:24 NLT**

Yet we know that a person is made right with God by faith in Jesus Christ, not by obeying the law. And we have believed in Christ Jesus, so that we might be made right with God because of our faith in Christ, not because we have obeyed the law. For no one will ever be made right with God by obeying the law. **Galatians 2:16 NLT**

41. The new creature doesn't need remission (the washing away or blotting out of) of sins, but forgiveness. Remission takes place first before forgiveness, remission deals with nature, the root cause of sin, while forgiveness deals with the acts of sin. The mere man needs the remission of sin, because his sins have to be washed away or blotted out by the blood of Jesus Christ.

For the life of a creature is in the blood, and I have given it to you to make an atonement for your souls upon the altar, since it is the lifeblood that makes atonement. **Leviticus 17:11**

And almost all things are by the law purged with blood; and without blood is no remission. **Hebrews 9:22**

In whom we have redemption through His blood, the forgiveness of sins according to the riches of His grace. **Ephesians 1:7**

42. The new creature is blessed with all spiritual blessings in the heavenly realms. The spiritual blessings of God are not accorded to the mere man because he is still in the state of sin.

    Blessed be God and the Father of our Lord Jesus Christ, who has blessed us with all spiritual blessings in heavenly places in Christ. **Ephesians 1:3**

    And God raised us up with Christ and seated us with Him in the heavenly realms in Christ Jesus. **Ephesians 2:6**

    His purpose was that now, through the church, the manifold wisdom of God should be made known to the rulers and authorities in the heavenly realms. **Ephesians 3:10**

43. The new creature is bold and has access to God, placing demands to God on his inheritance by faith, in regards whatever he desires, including wisdom or forgiveness. The mere man can come boldly to receive remission of his sin, and the qualify to have access to the Father in the name of Jesus.

In Him and through faith in Him we may enter God's presence with boldness and confidence. **Ephesians 3:12**

For through him, we both have access by one Spirit to the Father. **Ephesians 2:18**

Let us therefore come boldly to the throne of grace, that we may obtain mercy, and find grace to help in time of need. **Hebrews 4:16**

44. The new creature is an oracle of God. He is called to preach the word of God to the lost world. The word of God in His mouth is God speaking. The mere man cannot speak as God's oracle, he needs to be born again.

    No longer do I call you servants, for a servant doesn't know what his master is doing; but I have called you friends, for all things that I heard from My Father I have made known to you. **John 15:15**

    If anyone speaks, let him speak as the oracles of God. If anyone ministers, let him do it as with the ability which God supplies, that in all things God may be glorified through Jesus Christ, to whom belong the glory and dominion forever and ever. Amen. **1 Peter 4:11**

For though by this time you ought to be teachers, you need someone to teach you again the first principles of the oracles of God, and have come to need milk and not solid food. **Hebrews 5:12**

45. The new creature knows the revelations of God, and these revelations happen because he hath received from the Lord the Spirit of power, and of love, and of sound mind. The mere man has the spirit of fear in and around him. He cannot have the revelations of God because he is not His.

    For you did not receive a spirit of slavery that returns you to fear, but you received the Spirit of sonship, by whom we cry, "Abba Father!" **Romans 8:15**

    For God has not given us the spirit of fear; but of power, and of love and of sound mind. **2 Timothy 1:7**

46. The new creature is anointed, this anointing comes from the Holy Spirit who dwells in him. The mere man can't have the Holy Spirit; therefore, His anointing is not in him.

    The Spirit of Truth. The world cannot receive Him, because it neither sees Him nor knows Him. But you do know Him, for He abides with you and will be in you. **John 14:17**

But the anointing which you have received of Him stays in you, and you need not that any man teach you: but as the same anointing teaches you all things, and is truth, and is no lie, and even as it has taught you, you shall abide in Him. **1 John 2:27**

We have not received the spirit of the world, but the Spirit who is from God, that we may understand what God has freely given us. **1 Corinthians 2:12**

47. The new creatures are the custodians of the Word of God in the earth. They have the responsibility to teach, preach and pass on the word of God to the next generation. The mere men, cannot be custodians of the Word of God.

And now, brethren, I commend you to God, and to the word of his grace, which is able to build you up, and give you an inheritance among all them which are sanctified **Acts 20:32**

Let a man so account of us, as of the ministers of Christ, and stewards of the mysteries of God. Moreover, it is required in stewards, that a man be found faithful. **1 Corinthians 4:1-2**

We have also a more sure word of prophecy; whereunto you do well that take heed, as to a light that shines in a dark place, until the day dawns, and the day star arises in your hearts. **1Peter 1:19**

And the things that thou hast heard of me among many witnesses, the same commit thou to faithful men, who shall be able to teach others also. **2 Timothy 2:2**

48. The new creature has a mandate from the Lord to win the world of mere men back to God. The mere man is lost and the mandate is to reach and win him back to God.

Therefore, go and make disciples of all nations, baptizing them in the name of the Father, and of the Son, and of the Holy Spirit. **Matthew 28:19**

And He said unto them, go you into all the world, and preach the gospel to every creature. **Mark 16:15**

You have not chosen Me, but I have chosen you, and ordained you, that you should go and bring forth fruit, and that your fruit should remain: that whatsoever you shall ask of the Father in My name, He may give it you. **John 15:16**

49. The new creature is a king and a priest to his God. God made him so by the provisions of salvation. The mere man is a sinner, his works are an abomination before God.

And He has made us kings and priests to God and His Father; to Him be glory and dominion forever and ever. Amen. **Revelation 1:6**

You also, like living stones, are being built into a spiritual house to be a holy priesthood, offering spiritual sacrifices acceptable to God through Jesus Christ. **1 Peter 2:5**

But you are a chosen people, a royal priesthood, a holy nation, a people for God's own possession, to proclaim the virtues of him who called you out of darkness into his marvelous light **1Peter 2:9**

50. The new creature lives and walks by faith (which is the realm of God of all possibilities). The mere man walks by sight, (which is the realm of fear, controlled by the devil) the realm of limitations.

    For we walk by faith and not by sight. **2 Corinthians 5:7**

    So we fix our eyes not on what is seen, but on what is unseen. For what is seen is temporary, but what is unseen is eternal. **2 Corinthians 4:18**

    Now Faith is the substance of things hoped for, the evidence of things not seen. **Hebrews 11:1**

51. The new creature is hated by the world, just as the world hates Christ. The mere man is loved by

the world because he belongs to the world and its systems.

If the world hates you, understand that it hated me first. **John 15:18**

But they will treat you like this on account of My name, because they do not know the One who sent Me. **John 15:21**

52. The new creature practices righteousness because righteousness is his by nature. The mere man practices evil and abomination. The acts of his righteousness are as filthy rags before God.

    But we are all as an unclean thing, and all our righteousness are as filthy rags; and we all do fade as a leaf; and our iniquities, like the wind, have taken us away. **Isaiah 64:6**

    By this, the children of God are distinguished from the children of the devil: Anyone who does not practice righteousness is not of God, nor is anyone who does not love his brother. **1 John 3:10**

    We know that whoever is born of God sins not; but he that is begotten of God keeps himself, and that wicked one touches him not. **1 John 5:18**

Prayer of Salvation

If you have not been born again, I invite you to make Jesus Christ the Lord of your life by praying the following prayer and mean it from your heart:

> "O Lord God, I believe with all my heart in Jesus Christ, Son of the living God. I believe He died for me and God raised Him from the dead. I believe He's alive today. I confess with my mouth that Jesus Christ is the Lord of my life from this day. Through Him and in His name, I have eternal life; I am born again. Thank You Lord for saving my soul. I am now a child of God. Hallelujah"

Congratulations! You are now a child of God. To receive more information on how you can grow as a Christian, please get in touch with us through our website https://newcreationlifechurch.com/contact/

www.ingramcontent.com/pod-product-compliance
Lightning Source LLC
Chambersburg PA
CBHW070047100426
42734CB00039B/2184